Conversation with God

Conversation with God

A Christian Experience of Depression

DAVID C. WILSON

WIPF & STOCK · Eugene, Oregon

CONVERSATION WITH GOD
A Christian Experience of Depression

Copyright © 2020 David C. Wilson. All rights reserved. Except for brief quotations in critical publications or reviews, no part of this book may be reproduced in any manner without prior written permission from the publisher. Write: Permissions, Wipf and Stock Publishers, 199 W. 8th Ave., Suite 3, Eugene, OR 97401.

Wipf & Stock
An Imprint of Wipf and Stock Publishers
199 W. 8th Ave., Suite 3
Eugene, OR 97401

www.wipfandstock.com

PAPERBACK ISBN: 978-1-7252-6704-6
HARDCOVER ISBN: 978-1-7252-6705-3
EBOOK ISBN: 978-1-7252-6706-0

Manufactured in the U.S.A.   07/08/20

For Trish, now safe with her Lord,
who 'prophesied' the writing of this book.

Contents

Preface | ix

1. Thatcher's Children | 1
2. When Illness Strikes | 8
3. Christian Conversion | 16
4. Early Prayers | 24
5. Body Language | 33
6. Healings | 42
7. Hearing Voices? | 52
8. Kept Up All Night! | 60
9. Good Science—Bad Theology | 69
10. Old Truths—New Contexts | 79
11. Prophecy—The Old Testament Model | 89
12. Depression In The Old Testament | 97
13. Fasting—An Aid to Dialogue? | 107
14. Composite Prophecy | 115
15. Intimacy with God | 125
16. My Burden is Light | 133
17. In the Cool of the Day | 142

Authoritative Sources Consulted | 151

Preface

This book is about depression, which most people—if they think about it at all—consider it to be a medical condition treatable with modern drugs, and the medical analogy that underpins this viewpoint compares the diabetic's pancreas with the depressive's brain. The pancreas and the brain are just different organs of the body where, in the one case (diabetes) there is a shortage of insulin, and in the other (depression) a shortage of a different set of chemicals called neurotransmitters. Fix the shortage and the problem disappears, simple isn't it! The problem is, however, compounded by the 'psychosis' that appears to be the end result of certain experiences of depression, and which can lead to a person 'hearing voices,' or worse, 'seeing voices.' Psychosis may be seen as just one side of a coin the other side of which is mysticism, and surprisingly, 'seeing voices' is an entirely biblical experience (see chapter 12), but it usually fails to be translated as such because it does not make sense to us. In our post-modern, Western, biomedical world-view 'seeing voices' simply 'does not compute.' Although of necessity this book is to some extent autobiographical, my intention in writing it has been to bring these other features of depression to the attention of Christians, features that appear to be a wasted resource in our walk of faith. To a large extent Christians 'buy into' the secular world-view in which depression is often misunderstood as something from which the afflicted person "can snap out of." Perhaps, instead of pressing depressives to "pull themselves together," Christians should utilise them as a valuable resource in our corporate communication with God. But to do this raises serious questions concerning the current practices of our faith.

1

Thatcher's Children

As A CHILD I used to love stories, listening avidly to the Greek legends read to us at primary school and also to the Old Testament bible stories at the Baptist Sunday school I attended until the age of ten. At about that age I discovered temptation, when under the influence of 'friends,' I began to duck out of Sunday school, deciding instead to spend the threepence collection money on liquorice at the nearby herbalist shop. From that point on, and for a further thirty six years, I rarely graced the inside of a church building—save for births, marriages, and deaths, that is, the 'normal' and socially-required rites of passage. I set out on the great adventure of life becoming ever more determined to do exactly as I pleased but taking a long time to learn that life, or so it seemed, merely consisted of mutual, short-term reciprocity. One simply performed an appropriate number of transactions with other members of society in order to achieve one's desired goals, and the efficiency of this process determined the amount of success met with. Whilst inwardly accepting that this was the 'way the world worked,' I singularly failed to make the system work for me. For one thing, I enjoyed science and chose to begin work in manufacturing industry during the labor governments of the nineteen sixties, and Harold Wilson seemed to sum up my entire belief-system in his promise to bring about a "white hot technological revolution." The reality of course has been different, and in the post modern, post industrial society of today, the manufacturing sector has shrunk to perhaps a tenth of its previous size.

Having eventually qualified as a Chemist, however, I found I had other life-affecting problems, not least my impeccable timing, for I had managed to qualify during a major manufacturing recession. Finding a job when whole research departments are being closed is difficult to say the least, so I decided to train as a teacher, without it seems realising that those same redundant chemists were all doing the very same thing. It should have come as no surprise to find teaching posts in short supply when I began to apply for them twelve months later. The need to take stock of the situation pressed in upon me. I realized that I had spent fourteen years doing the wrong things at the wrong time, and the question which now arose was, should I add to my problems by seeking a teaching post in the wrong place? Being from the north west of England I was loath to uproot the four of us (for I had married and now had a wife and children to consider) and move to Hackney or the nether reaches of Glamorgan in order to teach. For the first time in my life I was compelled to reflect on 'the quality of life'—for want of a better phrase, and to decide in discussion with my wife, the direction our lives should take from now on.

Bereft

Now I was qualified to teach in schools, although I had been trained as a teacher of chemistry in further education, and it was a post in a college of further education or technology which I ideally sought. In the absence of such a post, the choice presented became one between teaching in a secondary school which might perhaps be at the other end of the country, or making a complete career break. I looked around for inspiration and saw what I thought was my salvation—I became an insurance agent! The attractions of this work for me lay in the relative freedoms it provided, since each working day comprised of a series of meetings with ordinary people during which I looked after their insurance needs and collected their premiums. No longer would I be trapped inside large organisations where advancement depended so much upon the interpersonal politics of the company or department, and with which I had so little facility. Instead I would be free, *almost* my own boss, and in my naivety I believed I had escaped the system–the enslaving matrix. As if to emphasize the irrevocable nature of this complete change of career, three days after accepting the insurance job I was offered sixteen teaching hours in a college of technology in south Manchester. Now sixteen hours is not a full post, it's about two thirds of a post and I was worried about the salary being enough, so I declined what would almost certainly have been 'a foot in the door.' Besides, there were other compelling reasons to remain an insurance agent. Firstly, the new job involved working out of an office in a town in East Cheshire, which was just far enough away from our home in Greater Manchester to qualify for financial assistance from the government towards removal expenses under a then current scheme. Secondly, and most importantly, the new employer was in financial services, and as such, offered discounted mortgages to its staff. This was vitally important because it permitted us to cross the North Manchester—South Manchester financial 'apartheid,' which normally prevented such movement. In other words, one normally needed a much higher salary, in order to migrate from the gloomy, industrial north to buy the more expensive houses of the leafy suburbs of South Manchester—or better still the towns and villages of East Cheshire. The net result was that I had contrived and manipulated my way into the 'good life' and I remained an insurance agent, going on to discover some very revealing things about both myself and the 'world' I thought I knew.

In the pre regulation Britain of the late nineteen-seventies it was possible to reply to an advertizement—usually one column-inch in length—in the local newspaper and get a job as an industrial branch, insurance agent without qualifications or experience of any kind in this work. As the name suggests the work involved the selling of life insurance to the 'industrial' or working classes, usually in their own homes with premiums being collected by the agent on a weekly basis. The insurance agent or 'clubman' was welcomed into homes on council estates and into terraced cottages throughout the land. He was the archetypal, bicycle-clipped, and anoraked individual who was so familiar on the streets of any British town of that era. Times were, however, changing and whole communities had been transplanted into satellite shire towns from the cities, by the slum clearances of the fifties and sixties. When combined with progressive deindustrialization, this produced massive social changes, not least, to sales of industrial branch, insurance policies. I had realized instinctively from my first day as an insurance agent, that there was a declining market for the weekly paid, industrial branch life policies, and so had concentrated upon sales of 'ordinary' branch life policies (collected monthly through the banking system), together with general or non-life policies. Gradually, this resulted in a great deal of free time since I found I could efficiently service my 'round' in little more than two days, leaving the remaining time available (theoretically) for new sales. In practice, however, I filled this time with innumerable hobbies and activities—anything to take my mind off my current situation.

That current situation involved a number of factors which in hindsight I have come to understand in total as a kind of bereavement, and I now understand that I was undergoing grief which did not diminish as the years passed by. But what, it may be asked, was I grieving for? It certainly wasn't the change in the 'status' of my current work compared with the scientific work done previously, and I felt no remorse for seemingly abandoning the fruits of my expensive education. In my refusal to remain in science, or at least in the teaching of science, I had it seems killed off my first love, my own potential, indeed my own becoming. Science had not simply been my work, it had been my belief-system, and I had believed in the new humanism based as it was on scientific materialism. I was now no longer intimately involved in that work with the consequence that I was floundering in grief as a result of a severed relationship with my erstwhile 'god.' I was learning the truth of the maxim "no man is an island" at first hand, and the gradual formation of new personal relationships with hundreds of clients, many of whom became friends, never completely alleviated these feelings.

Anger

Although the feelings of grief never went away, they could be anesthetized and this was done by means of furious activity, and numerous hobbies were indulged in, including winemaking, often five or ten gallons at a time, which on this scale dominated the house. Then there was the kit-car, which became a vast money-sink, the investments in stocks and shares which, although successful, didn't prove to be the big money-spinner hoped for, and all of these were accompanied by the perpetual DIY. Throughout this time the children were not exactly neglected or deprived so much as left to their own devices, for as a father I wasn't giving 100% and I knew it. Sundays were different, however, and the whole family as often as not would go walking on bits of the local Gritstone Trail—a footpath through the nearby Pennine foothills. As these walks continued and the seventies gave way to the eighties, I began to experience another emotional state which curiously only occurred during the walks, and in the very places where one would most expect to find peace I became angry. I spent those later walks in silence, seething with a resentment against the world in general for not realising my quintessential excellence, and my 'Micky Mouse' employer in particular for its insistence on pressing for sales of yesterday's financial products. In perfect hindsight of course, it seems quite natural to have expected grief to be followed by anger, an anger that more accurately highlighted my own unfulfilled potential. I was also angry with my wife, Chris, who was dragging me off on these walks when I really wanted to be planning ahead, checking my shares portfolio, working at something, anything, which would realize that lost potential. So as I walked, I inwardly fumed until the anger gave way to a determination to change things—once and for all. It should be understood that the angry determination of these walks was an internal state, which did not spill over into nastiness or unpleasantness towards either Chris or the kids. Indeed, it led eventually to a constructive dialogue with Chris about our future, as we worked out our plans to go into self-employment.

Status

We struggled for a long time over precisely what we were going to do in self-employment, before Chris agreed to join me in opening an insurance brokerage. Such a venture permitted me to employ the accumulated expertise of the past few years, years during which I had made a specialism of general branch insurance. Things didn't turn out the way we expected, however, and our new office took just 20 pence for photocopying in its first week's trading. Instead of doing business 'off the street' I found it necessary to continue to make personal calls on clients, who, if I were able to help them with their car or house insurance, would usually reward me with purchases of the more lucrative financial products. I discovered to my great surprise that I could sell, indeed had to sell to survive, and that this was linked to a more fundamental self understanding in that I was at last in a meaningful relationship with society by contributing my new expertise to it. I was amazed to discover, moreover, that the world had finally sat up and taken notice of us, seemingly because we had opened an office and I had exchanged my anorak for a three piece suit. The practising of my new 'profession' was finally allowing the grief and anger of the past few years to subside, especially as clients and even friends and family began to look on us in a new light. In the space of six or seven years I had experienced a roller coaster ride in terms of status, as I had moved from professional chemist/teacher to insurance agent before 'ascending' once more to the dizzy heights of self-employed broker. All this was of course taking place against the Thatcher backdrop of support, acclaim, and praise for entrepreneurial activities, and although our ascendancy seemed archetypally Thatcherite, the thought never crossed our minds that we might be included amongst those who would come to be called Thatcher's children. Thatcher's children included the 'Hoorah Henrys' and the 'Yuppies' (young and upwardly mobile), and I suppose we could have been described as 'Yuppies' if it hadn't been for the fact that I was fast approaching forty. Upwardly mobile we remained, however, and we demonstrated this to all and sundry by buying a huge, stone-built house with a correspondingly huge mortgage. The mortgage could not be justified by any multiple of our non-existent accounts, and derived from a liaison with the hungry and aggressive manager of a newly opened building society branch office. So there we sat, kings of the hill—the house was in fact called 'Springmount'—apparently set up for life and even discussing early retirement.

Regulation—The Theft of an Industry

In the early nineteen eighties some sixty five percent of the retail financial services industry—then known as the life assurance industry—lay in the hands of small firms of brokers. There were perhaps twelve and a half thousand such firms, usually comprising two or three partners, and whose combined business was worth many billions of pounds a year in new business fees and commissions. Many of these were composite brokers like our own firm, combining sales of financial products with general insurance sales. Sadly it seems, the wind of change is always blowing, and if a way could have been found to wrest this billion pound market from their hands, then the 1986 Financial Services Act was that way. The analogy, which springs to mind for this process, is the way in which the big supermarkets relieved the thousands of small grocers of their market share in the fifties and sixties. The grocers succumbed to the supermarkets whose massive buying power enabled them to undercut prices. Unlike the grocers, however, the brokers could compete on price with the big banks, building societies, and direct-selling insurance companies—their main competitors, and were consequently safe from this 'fair' form of competition. Businesses are, however, not only sensitive to price pressures, they are also vulnerable to cost pressures, and the onset of regulation under the new act brought about a massive yet *disproportionate* increase in business operating costs for the small brokerage. Although staggered over several years, the costs rose inexorably, beginning with the self-regulatory fees of several thousand pounds per year, and progressing with the enforced implementation of new systems and the quadrupling of paperwork. The new compliance visits to clients brought about a doubling or trebling of servicing costs, before finally the imposition of the requirement that all brokers (now called financial advisors) must obtain qualifications in financial services, ratcheted costs up further.

None of this could be done in a political vacuum of course, and the blind hatred of the 'chattering classes' for the commission based remuneration system of the industry provided the necessary political pressure. It is interesting to note that as I write, I do so to the anguished squeals of pain from policyholders of the famous, *non-commission* paying office, the Equitable Life, many of whom were led to believe (by an antagonistic media) that a life office's financial strength lay in its refusal to pay commission to sales staff. In any event, the result was brutal, and in the decade commencing in 1986 fully ten thousand financial services firms went out of business. From the politician's viewpoint it might have seemed that the sacrifice of such a 'small' lamb gave great political gains without actually damaging the wider public interest. After all, the same financial products would still be available from the same financial services companies, the only difference being that the financial advisors dealing with the public would now be 'accountable' employees. Events have shown the error of such thinking, for at the turn of the century the financial services industry bathes in a sea of blood, as companies cannibalize each other for a bigger piece of a shrinking market. The efforts of these companies are now almost exclusively directed towards the five million people who hold capital of fifty thousand pounds or more— not including their domestic properties, to the detriment of those of more modest means.

The death throes of the small 'grocers' of the financial services industry lay as a backdrop to our own problems. Unfortunately, it was an interactive backdrop, for not only did it impose punitive increases in our costs, it pervaded the atmosphere of the industry and distorted all planning for the future. It was about this time that Chris first became ill, and it is arguable that the additional stresses imposed upon us by the regulators contributed significantly to that illness.

2

When Illness Strikes

A LONG AND COMPLICATED buying 'chain' delayed the move to the new house, and it wasn't until the late autumn that we moved in. We had moved to the foothills, some four hundred feet above the town, and we soon discovered why towns are built in sheltered valleys as we experienced the first of two of the hardest winters we have ever known. Although the house sat in the lee of one end of a hilly ridge which protected it from the prevailing westerly winds, it was thoroughly exposed to the many easterlies which blew during those winters. Exposure to weather is, of itself, not a great problem, but when the blizzards came from the east they found ready access into the house because of its history and construction. The house had belonged in the past to a silk mill owner, and was essentially a Victorian extension of a pair of older cottages. Unlike the solid floors of the earlier cottages, suspended wooden flooring was used in the extension, and the floorboards used, although three inches thick (8cm.), were unrebated, that is, were simply laid side by side. Subsequently, modern air-bricks had been fitted to the east-facing walls of the extended part of the house below floor level, presumably in an attempt to remove the smell of dampness, with the result that an easterly wind could blow directly up into the house. The net effect was surreal, for we would often find ourselves sat in the lounge clad in overcoats, watching the carpet rise and fall in the centre of the room, as if by levitation. It was an experience we will never forget.

Burning the Candle at Both Ends

Mortgage multiples are not theoretical calculations done by building society managers in their spare time, rather, they are designed to prevent financial hardship, and we found we simply couldn't afford that house. At least, we couldn't afford to renovate it at that stage in the growth of our business, and we were obliged to do major building work ourselves on a DIY basis, which should more properly have been undertaken professionally. This work would be conducted at the weekends because the weekdays were occupied with the business. In my own case the business required the making of house calls for the selling of financial products in the evenings, thus lengthening the working day, but in Chris's case the situation was far more complex. Although I had failed to notice, Chris was now wearing a number of hats including those of secretary, receptionist, typist, bookkeeper, and debugger of our newly installed and very expensive computer system. In addition to this unfair distribution of work, the business was reaching a critical size, for an experienced business friend had told us, that when a venture of any kind exceeds three hundred clients, it becomes difficult for two people to manage it alone. Chris clearly needed extra time to complete her many tasks and decided to do the bookkeeping at home, after the office had closed, and while I was elsewhere seeing clients.

Unfortunately, this proved not to be a solution, since the bookkeeping simply became another hat for Chris to wear in a different arena. Whilst I was elsewhere, the domestic front involved Chris in numerous activities, including those of mother, cook, and of course housekeeper in a house four times larger than the previous one. To complicate matters still further, we had at about this time, become involved with the local Sea Cadet Unit. Both our teenage sons had joined the organisation, which was a small one run largely with the voluntary help of the parents of the children. Sadly, however, one of the individuals involved in leadership had an unerring talent for alienating many of these helpers, and as is so often the case in such circumstances, the workload begins to fall on fewer and fewer shoulders. We soon found ourselves amongst the few and whilst I became a committee member, Chris picked up two more hats becoming both the secretary and an officer in charge of the girls section. The competition for Chris's time was now severe both during the week when the Unit met twice in the evening, and most weekends when either parades or outward-bound type activities filled the time. In such a pressured situation it was inevitable that something would suffer, and as any self-employed businessman will confirm, it is frequently the bookkeeping and accountancy side of a business which bears the brunt of such pressure. Both of us, but Chris especially, now found ourselves on a seven-days-a-week carousel from which neither could alight, and subject now, to the background stresses of neglected bookkeeping and the fast encroaching and pervasive regulation of our business. Time was borrowed from everywhere and even our sleep was not sacrosanct, as our frenetic social life frequently found us locked inside public houses until two or three in the morning.

Post-Viral Syndrome—"Yuppy Flu"

When we did get time at home, the refurbishment work on the house would progress to a pattern, wherein a room would be 'gutted,' and this would often be followed by structural alterations, before finally being redecorated. As a consequence, the house was continually filled with house dust, cement dust, mites, horsehair (in the old plasterwork), mould, condensation, and paint. Moreover, the first job had been the application of a kerosene based pesticide to all exposed timbers as a woodworm preventative, causing one family member to remark that Chris was 'never the same from that time onwards.' Additionally, throughout this whole period, the oil-fired Rayburn cooker was burning continuously, and would blow back fumes into the house under certain weather conditions. This, we later discovered, was due to another peculiarity in the construction of the house, in particular the construction of the chimneys, which were all built below the level of the roof apex. The net effect of this was that negative pressure across the chimney pot under certain wind conditions caused blowback. In summary, almost every conceivable allergen was present in large quantity at Springmount at this time, along with toxic fumes and chemicals, all of which were present together in a cold and damp environment. It is my belief that Chris was sensitized by these substances during those early years, and that this permitted the later development of food allergies and food intolerance.

In hindsight, the picture of this period which comes to mind, is one of a stage performer trying to keep a dozen plates all spinning on canes at the same time. Clearly, the plates represent all the various activities undertaken, and there is a quite definite and practical limit to how many of these can be attempted at one time. Chris, however, had become the motivator of the totality of our lives, the initiator of new ventures and would admit of no such limit. When the first virus struck her during the Easter of 1988, Chris was obliged to drop everything, if only because it had settled on her chest, activating her asthma and leaving her completely breathless. It was of course merely the flu, and should respond eventually to the cocktail of steroids and antibiotics the doctor had prescribed, provided Chris rested and allowed herself to recuperate. Rest she did and for almost two weeks she was a captive of the lounge sofa, scarcely able to move, and taking little, if anything, in the way of food.

After two weeks the courses of medication came to an end, and although the asthma emergency was over, the flu symptoms failed to clear up and Chris was left with persistent temperature fluctuations, fatigue, tiredness, joint pain, and myalgia. More worrying, however, was another strange and menacing condition that affected her senses of taste and smell. In particular, her sense of smell had become so heightened in intensity, that food became nauseous to her and slowly, yet remorselessly, she reduced her food intake. A little over twelve months later Chris weighed six and a half stone. Looking back, it seems clear that Chris had been suffering from what was then uncomprehendingly called "Yuppy Flu," and was more properly known as Post-Viral Syndrome or M.E., but this was never medically diagnosed as such at the time. Nowadays the disease is known as Chronic Fatigue Syndrome (CFS or CFIDS in the USA), having been referred to by early researchers as 'the disease of a thousand names,' and popularly called "Yuppy Flu" because of its association with the young, city 'workaholics' of the eighties Thatcher scene. During this period the popular press would often carry stories of how the mysterious "Yuppy Flu" was afflicting the wealthy young foreign-exchange dealers in the city of London. Unfortunately, the media spotlight failed to pick out the many thousands of other (largely) professional people, whose lives were being destroyed by this debilitating illness. doctors, nurses, and teachers were among the many professionals so afflicted.

Chronic Fatigue Syndrome is a multifactorial disease, and it can present with both physical and psychiatric symptoms, and hospital-based studies have shown that over 50% of CFS patients meet the diagnostic criteria for major depression. Unfortunately, in such circumstances it has often been the case that in the absence of a definable physical cause, many patients were diagnosed as clinically depressed. Non-specialist General Practitioners were being asked to differentiate between CFS and depression, and in a situation where little was known about the former, it was common to label the physical symptoms as the psychosomatic outworkings of major clinical depression. It was precisely this situation which Chris encountered subsequent to that first viral attack, as she visited the doctor ever more frequently to complain of 'pains and fatigue.' The visits to the doctor were of course complicated in Chris's case by the additional 'weird' symptoms of heightened senses of smell and taste, which might have suggested an enhanced sensitivity to allergens, and this, together with repeated viral attacks, should have indicated that all was not well with her immune system.

To be fair, sufferers usually insist that the symptoms they experience have an *exclusively* physical cause, and are often so convinced of this, that their doctors are persuaded to arrange extensive physical examinations, that can even include endoscopic searches. This latter kind of examination usually produces little in the way of a result, leaving the medical consultant exasperated, and the G.P. 'out-of-his-depth' and embarrassed about having made a seemingly pointless referral. The truth is that CFS is holistic in nature, and is unexplained by primary physical or psychiatric causes.

Consequences

The physiological symptoms of CFS are not life threatening, nor are they of indefinite duration, for sufferers do recover, albeit often five, ten, or fifteen years on from inception. Unfortunately, long term illnesses of this nature, together with the associated, entrenched psychiatric problems, have far-reaching effects on sufferers' lives and (to use that dreadful word!) 'lifestyles.' Afflicted professionals, such as doctors or teachers are initially able to use up extensive paid sick leave, but find ultimately that they are compelled to give up their careers. It tends to be axiomatic that the busiest, most effective, *professional* people fall prey to CFS. The busy life in laboratory, surgery, or classroom becomes inexorably reduced in scope, until finally, in the worst cases, the sufferer is scarcely able to cross a room without the most excessive effort and pain. Usually, alongside and inextricably bound up with this remorseless advance into incapacity, comes a complete upheaval in the individual's personal values. Additionally, the individual's perception of role and status within both the family unit and wider society, undergo an enforced and painful realignment. Andrew Ferguson quotes the German theologian, Jurgen Moltmann, who identifies the problem precisely when he remarks: "If health is taken as a supreme value, it may lead to the suppression of illness and that 'the sick are pushed out of the life of society.' An individual who becomes seriously ill may lose his or her sense of their own worth."

Financially, the sufferer's household is obliged to endure trauma of unprecedented proportions, as two often substantial salaries, become—in the more fortunate cases—one small, early, retirement pension, plus various disability benefits. Such financial strictures bring with them an enforced humility, which may prove to be a difficult psychological burden to bear. The value of the sufferer's whole family unit may be seen to plummet in the 'eyes of society,' as two 'involved' professionals (perceived as net contributors) become 'carer' and 'cared for' respectively (both perceived as net beneficiaries). Children, teenagers especially, are without doubt traumatized by the complete reversal of fortunes, as houses, schools, and friends change in the kaleidoscope of stress-filled days passing before them. Adversity can, of itself, bring about aberrant behavior in the young.

At the outset of the illness, sufferers from Chronic Fatigue Syndrome usually become aware of physical symptoms such as muscle and joint pain, fatigue, sleep disturbance, abdominal discomfort, and body temperature fluctuations, but there is a second set of symptoms which are of potentially greater significance. This group comprises sheer mental incapacity of a completely debilitating order, invariably including impairment of memory, a persistent lack of concentration, and often difficulty in comprehending the spoken word. Keyboard performance, that is, the use of a typewriter or word processor displays these problems in microcosm, where the work produced frequently contains omissions and repetitions, and where work sessions are severely curtailed, perhaps restricted to only thirty minutes duration. Most professionals and business people struggle 'manfully' on in the face of physical pain and discomfort, given that their work is often sedentary and of a cerebral nature, but they are simply unable to function in the face of such mental incapacity. It is arguably this latter group of symptoms which terminate so many professional careers, and was certainly responsible for Chris's long, slow slide into firstly anorexia, and secondly depression.

We were later to discover that anorexia—as a symptom of CFS— is encountered by up to forty percent of sufferers albeit as a minor one. Indeed there are two so-called minor symptoms of CFS—nausea and *anorexia*— which have been suggested as strengthening the CDC (United States Centers for Disease Control and Prevention) case definition of CFS. In actual fact the anorexia exhibited by CFS sufferers is true anorexia (from the Greek meaning no appetite), and for Chris this was manifested as an absence of appetite due to masking by the associated CFS symptom of nausea, which itself was a function of her enhanced sense of smell. The anorexia displayed by Chris, in this first year of her illness, is to be contrasted with the 'usual' presentation wherein the 'normal' sufferer is very very hungry indeed—despite protestations to the contrary. From the initial 'triggering' of the illness by that first viral attack, it took fully fifteen months for Chris to reach a weight of six and a half stone. It was then that concerned family and friends suggested that a holiday—the first in six years—might be just 'what the doctor ordered.' In fact, it was precisely the opposite of the doctor's advice.

Anorexia Nervosa

What the doctor now saw, correctly as it turned out, was that the anorexia associated with CFS had now in fact become anorexia nervosa, that is, the so-called slimming disease most frequently associated with young girls. There had been a seamless transition from a minor symptom of CFS to a psychiatric illness in its own right, one which has the highest mortality rate of all such illnesses. The doctor's advice was against travelling, and the coach journey to southern France was a painful one for the six and a half stone, yet undismayed Chris. Nothing could have shown Chris's deterioration over the past twelve months more clearly than that holiday. The sight of this thin, milk, white figure in a blue sun-hat, who spent too much time in the toilets, was completely out of place amongst the healthy, bronzed Europeans relaxing by the camp pool. Because we were holidaying with two other couples—our close friends—we had between us half a dozen kids, and this meant a great deal of time was spent eating socially as a group. Now social eating causes anorexics great problems, especially in restaurant situations, for despite careful and judicious selection from the menu, it is rarely possible to control portion size. The remedy is found in impromptu exits to the toilets in order to vomit, or if all else fails, the taking of laxatives to relieve fictitious constipation. It was quite remarkable how that holiday brought the true situation home to everyone, for it was impossible for Chris to conceal anything, with friends so close by most of the time.

Questions were on everyone's mind: How had this condition arisen? What did this woman in her early middle years have in common with the teenagers who more commonly succumb to this illness? Indeed, the prognosis was bad, for there is even less chance of recovery for sufferers in their later years, than there is for younger ones. A clue to causation lies in Moltmann's comment about the way in which a person's self-worth may plummet during serious illness. Chris had been the linchpin of the family, holding together every facet of the whole enterprise, including business, home, and leisure interests. In the long aftermath of that initial virus attack, Chris had been obliged to 'carry on' whilst constantly feeling ill, and quite naturally her performance—her ability to get things done—had suffered as a consequence. Despite begging her to let something go, such as giving up her work with the Sea Cadets, she insisted on trying to maintain her life in all its aspects to the fullest extent, and failure to do so for a perfectionist such as Chris, can have only one outcome. Unable to function properly, Chris convinced herself that she simply wasn't 'up to the job,' and in common with other anorexics she lost all sense of her own self-worth. Low self-worth is the common factor shared by all anorexics, both young and old, and the anorexic response to that (wrong-headed) realisation and false self-understanding is also a common one. Anorexics respond by controlling the only thing that they feel is still within their control—their bodies. In the case of young girls, restriction of food intake results ultimately in an arrest of menstruation, with the result that control is imposed upon the biological changes normally brought about during puberty. Effectively, control is imposed upon the (unwanted) arrival of womanhood with all its attendant life changes. In like manner, Chris imposed control upon her own body, as a substitute for the control she now felt she had lost, or was losing over her life. With our return to France had come the full, awful realisation that Chris was now living out an anorexic lifestyle, a lifestyle which had up to that point remained largely concealed.

3

Christian Conversion

WE RETURNED HOME FROM holiday to a world that was fast changing, and as the decade gave way to a new one, talk of slowing growth and recession, was in the air. At the very time when it became noticeably harder to make sales of the financial products so essential to profitability, Chris's contribution to the business had diminished to almost zero. Two almost opposing factors were now combining to keep Chris out of the office. Firstly, there was the leaden fatigue and myalgia which is such a defining feature of CFS, and which tied her to her bed until late each morning. Secondly, there was the hyperactivity which can come to dominate the life of an anorexic approaching the latter stages of semi-starvation, and that for Chris, was manifested as three and sometimes five mile walks into the office. Physiological starvation produces significant changes in the brain, reducing neurotransmitter levels in particular, and some animal studies have indicated that hyperactivity could help to reverse this effect. Put simply, hyperactivity could be viewed as a defensive, almost involuntary mechanism, helping to minimize the effects of starvation. In any event, the combined effect of the CFS and the anorexia was that Chris would often turn up at the office towards the middle of the afternoon, invariably leaving again quite soon afterwards because her concentration span was so limited. These two opposing physical effects were, however, to pale into insignificance when compared to another outcome of both illnesses.

As noted already, many sufferers from Chronic Fatigue Syndrome meet the diagnostic criteria for major depression. Likewise, anorexics as a result of the changes to brain chemistry they undergo, invariably suffer from depression in the later stages of semi-starvation. Depression, although not proven to be a direct cause or product of eating disorders, is invariably found associated with them, so much so, that the eating disorders have latterly been described as the 'new depression' of the late twentieth century. The vagueness with which depression is linked to the eating disorders is matched by a similarly inexact link with brain chemistry, and with serotonin in particular. Serotonin is a chemical messenger (neurotransmitter) in the brain that is linked with mood and consciousness as well as with eating, sleeping, and sex. Depression is linked with a deficiency of serotonin and may also be linked to obsessive illnesses such as binge eating. As a sufferer from both CFS and anorexia nervosa Chris would have a high probability of also suffering from major depression, but this only became apparent later on through perfect hindsight.

I still had implicit faith in the medical profession at this time, and with Chris maintaining that all her problems stemmed from her enhanced senses of smell and taste, I arranged for her to be admitted to a private hospital at my own expense. Shortly before admission Chris's depression had become critical and she had begun to express suicidal intent. When this continued during her stay in hospital, a decision was taken to detain her under section 3 of the Mental Health Act 1983 in order to protect her from self-harm. The effect of section 3 is to make a period of detention of up to six months available to the medical staff, during which they can both assess and treat the patient. Paying for a few weeks private care while tests were carried out was one thing, but the prospect of funding a stay of up to six months was quite out of the question. I was immediately obliged to make arrangements for Chris to be transferred to our local NHS hospital, and within two weeks of her admission to the local psychiatric hospital, she had been detained under section 3.

Fortunately, the NHS still had dedicated psychiatric hospitals in most towns at that time, usually set in spacious and beautiful grounds, but tending to group together patients with widely differing complaints. At least Chris was able to enjoy the therapeutic effect of the late summer weather in those gardens, before they came to be sold off to a housing developer and replaced by a so-called 'secondary unit' in the nearby general hospital. In addition to her 'escapes' into the grounds, Chris actually did escape from the premises on one or two occasions, for she so hated the enforced confinement and pressured food regimes. Inevitably she was returned to hospital by the police, and began to 'plot' a more permanent exit by 'cooperating' with the 'programme.' The psychiatric treatment programme was twofold in its approach, consisting of the administration of antidepressant drugs to combat the depression, together with what was basically a feeding schedule. At first, Chris had refused to take part in that schedule, using every ruse imaginable to trick the staff into believing she was complying. Eventually, however, she realized she must eat, and eat substantially, in order to get out and to get home. I was enlisted to bring huge quantities of bananas into hospital for Chris, who throughout, still insisted her heightened sense of smell prevented her from eating much else. Apart from the bananas and toast, which she could tolerate, she ate little else, and on these alone her weight increased to eight stone plus, a point at which the staff considered her 'safe.' Chris was discharged shortly before Christmas, after spending only three months detained under section 3, but bringing the total time spent in both hospitals to nearly five months.

Despair

Sadly, the whole thing had been a ruse, a means to an end which, once achieved, allowed Chris to continue her anorexic lifestyle in peace. The truth was that nothing had changed and semi-starvation, hyperactivity and weight loss resumed as the new year unfolded, despite a number of new factors entering the equation. Following discharge, Chris had been encouraged to take part in some of the activities at a local day centre, as a continuation of the occupational therapy which she had received whilst an in-patient. In Addition, she began to see a social worker for an hour's counselling each week at the local social services centre, and this, together with a weekly home visit from a second social worker put a much needed monitoring regime in place. The social workers befriended Chris, who responded to their counselling with intimate confidences about her innermost fears, seeming to make some headway with their help. In the face of remorseless continuing deterioration and the return of suicidal inclinations, it was the advice and counsel of these new friends, which persuaded Chris to agree to a voluntary re-admission to hospital in the early spring. Chris had believed that going into hospital was to be for a fortnight or so, but this is hardly ever the case with psychiatric admissions, and the fears of the social workers were soon confirmed as the following entry in her diary reveals:

> Had a bad night last night, intended to take the aspirin at about 9.30. I was very desperate, but the nurse saw this and sat and talked to me until about 2.45, when they put me to bed. She managed to talk me into giving her the aspirin and now I'm

regretting it already. Didn't sleep, had perhaps one hour all night. Now I'm very tired.

For fully two and a half months, the diary entries record the prevalence of persistent low mood, and towards the end of May, Chris discharged herself. Throughout June, the concerned social workers attempted to persuade Chris to return to the ward. Finally they succeeded, and by the middle of the next month Chris voluntarily admitted herself, before seemingly realising the pointlessness of it all and leaving again on the very next day. I was weary of it all, for although these voluntary admissions allowed much freedom—permitting for example, evenings and weekends to be spent at home—they were completely ineffectual, failing to alter either mood or behavior. I decided to bring Chris home for good, knowing full well that such a decision could have led to Chris's death, since a heart attack in her weakened anorexic condition was a distinct possibility. Nevertheless, come home she would, whether to live or to die.

The medical record of the late summer of 1991 shows that my (unilateral) decision to discharge Chris, and to subsequently block attempts to section her, had thrown both the medics and the social workers into consternation. The consultant psychiatrist made his fears known to the G. P. in a letter discharging Chris from his care, at the same time making clear his belief in the continued need for her "psychiatric management." Modern Western society will not permit individuals to make such life-determining, decisions against the collective wisdom of the medical profession, and in such circumstances, the system has remedies. When presented with this state of affairs the social services department considered invoking Section 29 of the Mental Health Act, which can be used to displace the nearest relative, "where consent is unreasonably withheld." Despite the advice of the social services department, and notwithstanding Chris's brief admission to Accident & Emergency following another overdose, the G. P., in whose primary care Chris now was, failed to act.

Throughout that autumn, and against this tragic background, I continued to struggle with the other problems, to which had been added the medical debts from the period Chris had spent in private care. We were now hopelessly behind with the accounts, financial services regulation was even more onerous, and we had been obliged to (prematurely) employ staff. The hiring of a general branch clerk to deal with an enlarged motor insurance account had become essential, but in terms of (wo)man power, our clerk had merely replaced Chris in the office, and at substantial further cost into the bargain. Interestingly, it came to light that our clerk's husband was a member of a well known, fraternal, and charitable fellowship, the same one it turned out, that I had joined a few years earlier. One of the major tenets of this fellowship is a professed belief in 'The Great Architect of the Universe,' and prior to initiation into membership, candidates are asked the question: 'Do you believe in God.' To answer this question in the affirmative forced a major turning point in my life, for I had always previously vocalized a kind of vehement, scientific atheism, loosely based on the theory of evolution. The examining committee had, of course, only wished to have me mouth the words in a compliant manner, but strangely, it had meant so much more to me than that. Now, in the hour of my greatest need, I found that this worldwide fellowship of brothers, was not so much unwilling, as unable to help us in our desperate situation—they were simply out of their depth.

The Feast of Christmas

Christmas had always been a difficult time of year for us ever since the death of Chris's father in the early eighties. With Stan's death, a central focal point of the wider family had gone, leaving no one among the four married daughters who felt either willing or able to assume the mantle of family head. All this meant disarray at Christmas, when social arrangements tended to be made in a tentative and half-hearted manner, frequently leading to mild upset of one form or another. In order to avoid such complications, we began to spend the Christmas holiday away from home. The Christmas this year was no exception, being the eighth such year spent away, and the four of us duly departed for a five day sojourn in a rented cottage in Wales. Winter in west Wales is, as often as not, a fairly mild affair and that week in Harlech proved to be one of the warmer ones, positively balmy in fact. Nevertheless we stocked up with coal, not so much for fear of harder weather or even for aesthetic effect, but more to combat the bodily coldness Chris was feeling due to her emaciation. The emotional pain of the past twelve months was now reaching a crescendo, as Chris combined her long-standing culinary skills with the anorexic tendency to constantly work with, and be around food, whilst avoiding eating much of it. Gradually one becomes accustomed to the tiny portions of food and the drinks of diet Coca Cola, but to be sat at the Christmas table—the table of plenty—and be served by an emaciated, five and a quarter stone anorexic is the most harrowing experience imaginable. At such a low weight Chris was constantly tired, and when this was reinforced by the C. F. S. symptoms, she was in the habit of taking frequent naps, and I would, like as not, take advantage of this time to venture out for an after dinner walk to think things through.

The Deal

The streets of the town were completely deserted (indeed there is nothing quite like a Welsh seaside town during the Christmas break for peace and quiet), as my mind turned over the seeming impasse of our situation. In the past I had always found it possible to solve every problem thrown up by the vicissitudes of life, for although a little introverted, I possessed confidence and courage of a sort, in good measure. We had begun a business on a shoestring budget, based on a partnership between two people who contributed different skills, both of whom had assumed that good health was a given, that would always be there. As long term illness encroached on our lives, the unanticipated costs of that illness had accrued to the business, which was now approaching a debt-ridden crisis point. All the possible solutions to our problems, such as the employment of domestic cooks and cleaners, or the hire of a bookkeeper and private nurse, seemed to involve yet more uncovered expenditure. I was beset on all sides not only by the regulators, but also by numbers of other creditors whose ranks had now been joined by the Revenue, and who distracted me from the sales and marketing so essential to continued earnings. As I walked along that deserted main road, I knew that I had reached the end of my capabilities, and I knew moreover, that nobody else could help me either.

It is well known that low light levels can have an adverse effect upon a person's mood, and I feel sure that the gloom of that late December day heightened the sense of despair I felt. As I continued to mull over the intractability of my problems, I noticed a small, stone church, slightly raised above the road, to my left. The churchyard seemed a yet quieter place—if that were possible—in which to think through my predicament, so I opened the gate and entered. Truth to tell, I felt like praying (for the first time in thirty plus years), or at least vocalising the situation to somebody–anybody. Expecting the church door to be locked, I was surprised when it yielded, giving me access to a very simple, empty church adorned only with a few children's drawings. High up on the wall at the far end of this one-room church, was a filled crucifix, which struck me as unusual for an Anglican church in congregational mid-Wales. To this figure of Jesus I spoke these words:

> I have no power to affect anything in my life, but you have the power. If you will help me, I will serve you.

No answer came, no still, small voice, indeed, having spoken these few words in the deadliest earnestness and sincerity; I simply turned on my heel and left the building. The only feeling I had as I walked back up the road to the cottage, was one of having done something concrete, something quite particular, and which made the 'after' different from the 'before.' Perhaps it was my imagination, perhaps it was hope, but I knew that a new factor was there now, which hadn't been there before.

Looking back on that moment, having had the benefit of five years of full time theological study, I still find myself amazed at those words, for I had somehow managed to condense most of both testaments of the bible into a couple of dozen words. To begin with—and most importantly—there was repentance, which at that time I thought simply meant an oft-repeated apology to God for ongoing sin. Now whilst it may mean that, it has a much more fundamental meaning involving a person's orientation towards God. Put simply, repentance is a once-for-all about face, in which a (wo)man makes the irrevocable decision to turn around from facing self to facing God. Sin is subsumed within that decision, which by its irrevocable nature, ensures that sin continues to be covered. It had always puzzled me that my words in the Harlech church contained no apology for, indeed no reference to sin, but this was because I had unwittingly renounced the fundamental 'sin' of Genesis 3:6—the 'sin' of disobedience. Then there was humility, for I had abased myself before God sharing this trait with Jesus himself, and combining this with an acknowledgement of, even fledgling trust in, God's superior ability to sort the mess out. Whatever we understand them to be, repentance and humility, together with an acknowledgement of God's power, are to be expected as par for the Christian course, but what of servility, is that too required? Twenty first century moderns could perhaps be forgiven for believing, that the slavery abolished two hundred years ago, plays no part in Christian conversion. Such a belief would, however, be based upon a false premise about slavery in the first centuries of the Christian era.

Fundamental differences exist between the wholly economic exploitation of the mainly African slaves of recent centuries, and the slavery of early Christian and pre-Christian times. The cruelty and grinding poverty which were so much a feature of the former, are largely absent from first century Romano-Greek culture, where slavery was not so much a vile oppression, as a means of organising society, and which, bizarre as it may sound, approximated to the social security system of the day. Indeed, many free men sold themselves into slavery in order to avoid starvation for themselves and their families. On this point, it was not unknown for slaves to buy themselves out of one form of slavery (e.g. heavy agricultural work), and then sell themselves into slavery within a domestic household. As a result they would become a family retainer, often developing a discrete skill or trade to the mutual benefit of themselves and their new masters. It was certainly the case that some people actually sold themselves into slavery in order to climb socially. Moreover, in the Roman *paterfamilias*, the Roman head of house(hold) treated his slaves and his own sons exactly alike, having in fact, the (legal) power of life and death over both. Against this background, Paul's exhortations to the Corinthians (1 Cor. 7:22) become a little clearer, especially when it is understood that very little difference existed between a slave and a freedman, since both owed exclusive duties of service to master and patron respectively. It is my belief, therefore, that slavery is part and parcel of the Christian life, and that my servility in Harlech was a needed, indeed essential part of the conversion act.

The whole thing became clearer still when I later realized that the Christ or Messiah was a king, and thus Christ*ians* were kingsmen or vassals. The word 'vassal' brings the argument full circle, since it derives from the Greek, *basileus*, (king). This seems odd really, until you realize that to our English ears, the Greeks, and indeed the Spaniards (but the other way round), mix up their 'v' and 'b' sounds. Moreover, all the great covenants or deals (for that is what a covenant is) of the Old Testament involved vassals. The great covenants of the faith recorded in scripture, are said to be modelled on suzerainty treaties, in which a Suzerain or regional super king offers his protection to lesser vassal kings, in return for tribute, as was the case with Nebuchadrezar's first incursion into Judah in 605 BC. Usually, these treaties were very workaday affairs, enabling life to go on in a normal fashion, and especially allowing cross-border trade to be conducted in an orderly manner.

Despite my overwhelming feelings of despair on that day in Harlech, I remember being consciously aware that the deal I had done had that same workaday feel about it—I had had the nerve to approach Almighty God with a proposition and He had accepted it without fuss. The realisation didn't dawn on me until much later on, that He has been doing this kind of thing for a very long time, and as with many others before me, it involved my trading everything that I was, or could become, not for my social security—as in Roman slavery, but rather for my eternal security. Following our return from Wales, I began to pray regularly, prayers which were short and to the point. I would usually pray kneeling beside the bath for the sake of privacy, since I had not spoken to anyone of this event, Chris included. Soon, things began to change.

4

Early Prayers

OUR RETURN FROM THE Christmas break in Wales was to a situation that had worsened further, and this centred upon the business premises we occupied at that time. Seven years after opening our office, we had been persuaded by our eloquent accountant to join him and another (bookkeeping) business, in renting a large Victorian house. The stated intention was the joint operation of a "financial services centre," by our two resident businesses and which would involve a kind of symbiosis, in which each firm would actively introduce business to the others. What actually transpired was very different, and eighteen months on from that decision very little new business had come our way. As the recession of the early nineties deepened, the atmosphere in the premises changed, and we realized that our role was a very different one to that discussed at the outset. The truth was that we were viewed simply as subtenants, intended to provide a useful subsidy towards the high rent of the property, and to bring an air of "busy . . . ness" to the place as a result of our much larger, established client base. Our offices were on the second floor, fully two flights of stairs removed from the ground floor reception desk, which was manned by the accountancy staff. Resentment, it seems, had been building up because of the need to sort the high volume of mail we received, and also because most of our visitors were insurance office inspectors requiring direction up the stairs to our offices. But a much more sinister reason lay behind the poisoned atmosphere which prevailed upon our return to work that January.

On the first day back I discovered that during our short, holiday absence, our offices had been entered, and the computer server had been turned off. Although this might seem inconsequential, we had been advised not to turn the machine off, because to do so (especially in those early days of office computing) could cause hard disc failure through what was called "cold booting." Confrontation with my antagonistic landlord now seemed inevitable and duly arrived one hour later. During that encounter I was advised that I had no rights to privacy, especially so, since my rent payment was (ten days) overdue. I realized that this heated exchange had been set up to raise this very issue of a missed rent quarter day, and the heinous crime of taking a Christmas holiday in such circumstances. If I had expected sympathy on account of Chris's illness I was to be disappointed, for in that same exchange she was accused of fouling the shared ladies toilets, and afterwards, it took us a full week to piece together the full import of what was going on. Throughout the previous year, Chris had been dragging her emaciated frame past reception, up those stairs and into our office under the gaze of our landlord and his staff, and they had been frightened by what they had seen. Fear, it turned out, was the motivating factor for all the antagonism we were receiving, and the name of that fear was AIDS. Chris's mysterious affliction had been labeled in ignorance, and she had been blamed for some unconnected incident in the ladies toilets, because of her anorexic tendency to use the toilets more frequently than is 'normal.' Events moved rapidly from this point on, and by the end of the week the toilets had been segregated on the basis of ignorant fear rather than gender, whilst the heating was cut off pending our payment of the rent. Such an irrevocable breakdown in inter-office relationships seemed to offer no prospect of an end to these frustrations, and our forced vacation of the premises seemed inevitable.

Every day, in the privacy of the bathroom I had been praying, praying for an end to this insoluble, and now worsened situation of trying to carry on working at the office. In circumstances where one's very spirit is being sapped by the hopelessness of continual illness, I prayed for help as I set my plans to vacate the offices. The first answer to prayer came in the form of a visit from a man who had just set up in the business of office relocation. It was a quite literal 'Godsend,' he dealt with everything from telephones to office furniture removal, and by the middle of February we were out of that place. Importantly, the actual move was achieved in complete secrecy across a single weekend—in order to avoid unpleasantness and perhaps further harassment—and we were able to leave those offices on Friday night, beginning work in our new location on Monday morning. On that morning, I found myself working in the huge attic room of our home; exactly the same place where in Victorian times, a previous owner of the house had operated his silk weaving machine. If our evacuation from the office in 'Dunkirk' style had been a second answer to prayer, then the wrath of our erstwhile landlord, seeking legal restitution for his perceived losses, would require further supplications to our new Helper.

Help Arrives

I can't remember those early prayers much, except to say that they were blunt, brief, and contained a lot of pleas for help. Although, I obviously prayed for help with our office problems, my predominant recollection of the time is of constantly praying for help for Chris, but without having any idea of the form such help could, or would take. Later on, I discovered that the number of people praying for Chris at about this time, eventually reached nine hundred or so, and amongst the first of those people, one in particular played a key role. Within the family, Chris had a special rapport with her sister Margaret, whose concern for Chris's predicament had prompted a discussion with a close friend. Margaret's friend had a Christian sister, who, on hearing the story, became 'burdened' with the need to pray for Chris's healing, and requested a meeting with, or visit to Chris—both of which were denied. Unable to meet with Chris, and finding her prayers for healing to be unsuccessful, she changed the tack of her prayers, praying instead for local Christians to contact Chris. At about the time of our relocation of the business, that contact came via a Christian friend of Chris's youngest sister, Janice. On hearing Chris's harrowing tale, Janice's friend, who was a member of a small (healing) prayer group, initially asked if the group could pray for her. Permission was given for this, but when a few weeks later the group asked to pray with Chris, her consternation was clear, and to consternation was soon added surprise, when she found her erstwhile agnostic husband actively encouraging her to meet these people. The agnostic, of course, professes to have no knowledge of God, and even the acknowledgement of theism, which had been required prior to joining my 'fraternal fellowship,' did not change that. Chris knew nothing of my secret vow in Harlech, and thought I was still an *ignoramus* (Latin equivalent of the Greek term: agnostic). Nevertheless she agreed to a first meeting with the group, whilst I thrilled with delight at the sheer improbability that this contact could ever have come about.

Conversion No. 2

In other words, I was delighted and amazed at the reality of answered prayer coming in the form of an actual *healing* prayer group, all four of whom worshipped at a local Baptist church. As a new (secret) Christian of only six or eight weeks standing, and not having had any contact whatsoever with other Christians, I didn't even know that such things as healing prayer groups existed. Although I could not know it, these were, of course, significant times in Christian circles, following as they did, the John Wimber/Vineyard Movement visits to Britain. One of the John Wimber 'tours' had included a visit to a north of England church, which was pastored at that time by the current principal of Spurgeon's College, London, thereby engendering a fairly local Baptist connection and influence. In the perfect hindsight of a theological training, I now recognize the Wimber influence on this group of sincere, believing Christians, who for two years became a rock of support for Chris.

The group were brimming with enthusiasm and were avidly reading a wide selection of the popular, charismatic books that circulated at the time, especially those with an emphasis on healing. Looking back, it is clear that they anticipated fairly early success in the form of physical healing, but in this, they were to be largely disappointed, instead fulfilling another, very much needed function. Apart from the first two or three meetings, the group met with Chris at our home where the chief result of their prayers, was the indescribable feeling of peace that she experienced. The peace of God (Phil. 4:7) was in fact guarding the thoughts of Chris's mind (heart) from the psychological troubles of her anorexia. Again and again, Chris met with the group simply in order to experience that peace, and it was this that, in part, ultimately led to her commitment to Christ. It was about four weeks into these meetings with the prayer group that I disclosed to Chris my own prior commitment to Christ, and how their involvement in our lives could only have been the result of prayer. Easter was early that year, and on April 1st. Chris committed her life to the LORD, later often remarking on the appropriateness of 'April fools day'. Interestingly, in her prayer of commitment she too struck a deal, for she had recently formed a friendship with a social worker, and asked the LORD to maintain that friendship outside its current professional confines. The prayer of commitment had been prayed from the heart privately, but in a subsequent meeting, the prayer group insisted that this was 'ratified' by being repeated aloud, adding in a more stylized line or two of 'normal' commitment prayer. In the following weeks, as we began to read our bibles, we felt it was incumbent upon us to meet with other Christians on a fairly regular basis, and so we became members of that same local Baptist church. But throughout, we never lost the specialness, which had derived from having made personal, almost unaided, commitments to the LORD.

Requesting the "Gifts"

From the outset of their Christian commitments, Western Christians suffer from almost insurmountable difficulties in their relationship with God, which derive entirely from their cultural heritage. Indeed, the whole emphasis of our culture rests upon the cult of the *individual*, whose prosperity and welfare are the mainspring of the policies of all the political parties, of whatever hue. Individualism is now to all intents and purposes, the single most virulent philosophy driving our society, holding metaphysical hands with those other modern philosophies, pluralism and humanism. The 'Enlightenment' which arguably began in the seventeenth century, and which has bequeathed huge advances in material prosperity, has also brought about an intellectual 'sea change,' profound in its consequences. In essence, the perception of self has changed, and the increasing sense of selfhood has been understood as the transformation of 'public man' into 'private man,' or *psychologisation*. The psychologisation process is, in effect, the internalisation of public, corporate man—once exemplified by external indications of rank such as clothing and apparel—into the modern individual known today. All this has consequences for Christians, who respond to their social nurturing by unwittingly placing undue emphasis upon their *individual* relationship with God, and this is particularly exemplified in their prayer life. It must be emphasized here, that the concept of an individual relationship is quite different from the concept of a *personal* relationship, and it remains one of the misfortunes of modern society, that this distinction has become so blurred. When acknowledging that Christians have a personal relationship with God, it is necessary to understand that this was intended to be lived out in a corporate environment, and personal prayer also took place primarily within that same environment. New Testament prayer was fundamentally a corporate activity, often to be found within households, that is, amongst (and between) families, and the fundamental unit of the family still remains the relationship between husband and wife.

In response to this shared heritage of social nurture as an individual, I prayed alone—as did Chris, although we did at least 'compare notes' from time to time. Amongst the prayers that we each prayed simultaneously yet separately, were prayers asking the LORD for specific gifts of the Spirit. We requested these gifts at the behest of the prayer group, who were imbued with the belief—then current in some charismatic circles—that one could request any combination of the spiritual gifts listed in 1 Corinthians 12. In other words, it was a kind of "pick 'n mix," and I remember requesting the gifts of wisdom and prophecy—not being too terribly interested in such things as administration—and I remember Chris saying she had also requested prophecy. In the event, we did not receive any giftings, at least, as we then understood them to be, and it wasn't until much later that I realized the truth of I Corinthians 12:11—God gives gifts as *He* determines!

Darkening Storm Clouds

If the evacuation of the offices had been our 'Dunkirk,' then we were now firmly ensconced inside 'Fortress Britain,' and our enforced mid-lease move soon began to have its consequences, as our erstwhile landlord and accountant engaged himself in furious legal activity. To begin with, we owed him a four-figure sum for the last set of accounts he had prepared, and having refused outright our offer of instalments, he began a civil action in the county court to recover the full amount. He sent his partner to represent him at the trial, and we both presented our cases to a surprisingly young presiding judge. The case was defended because I had counter claimed for the few hundred pounds owed to us on a separate matter by their firm. Needless to say, I had prayed fervently for help in this, my first encounter with the civil justice system, and was amazed when the judge ordered us to go into an annex room, in order to work out a repayment programme by instalment! Our counter claim was rejected by the judge, who regretfully pointed out that the monies owed to us, were owed by a different company belonging to our former landlord, and who then recommended that we begin a separate action.

Unfortunately, this action over accountancy fees was only the first skirmish in a long series of legal battles, and fairly soon after its resolution, our antagonist brought an action in the high court. Since we had left our subtenancy approximately half way through, we were being pressed for payment of eighteen months rent and our share of the utility costs, together with the associated legal costs and interest. In all, this amounted to a quite preposterous five figure sum, which, as is often the case, bore no relation to reality. Everything had happened so quickly, and rather than remain under what had become an oppressive, feudal regime at the old offices, we had executed a tactical withdrawal to a seemingly more defensible position—but was it? I knew that my tormentor had many connections with the local law firms, and I therefore decided to use a solicitor based some distance from the town. The defense I presented to our solicitor was based on the initial agreement to form a "financial services centre," and our erstwhile associate's failure to honor that agreement by not introducing new financial products sales leads to us. We had suspected that our adversary was placing financial products business elsewhere, but initially, we had very little in the way of hard evidence for this, and my interviews with our solicitor were very unfulfilling. Indeed, he seemed to spend most of the meeting trying to dissuade us from fighting, and my main recollection is of passing the time quite enthralled by his white, well-manicured hands. Nevertheless, we left the battle in what we thought were also his capable hands, only to receive a rude awakening one morning in the late summer.

When the bailiff knocked at the door we didn't know what to do, but were able to successfully protest that the case—so far as we were aware—had still not yet been resolved. Fortunately, the bailiff offered to return within a week to allow us the time to find out exactly what had transpired, and this despite holding an order to seize our goods. A telephone call to the solicitors office left us in a panic, for it seemed that our solicitor had simply failed to turn up at a court hearing—presumably an application for summary judgement—and in his absence, the judge had upheld the claimant's case. We were in the doldrums of despair, since we were not only facing an implacable enemy who was besieging us with weekly visits from the bailiffs, but in addition, now had to contend with a negligent solicitor. Naturally, we prayed, and were consoled by the perception from the LORD that "*your enemies are my enemies,*" indeed, as new Christians we were constantly surprised by how often this 'nice' New Testament God was expressing some very Old Testament sentiments. In this knowledge, we took steps to relieve the intolerable pressure we were under, by employing another firm of solicitors, making sure that this time they were 'up to the job.' To this day I still do not know how to evaluate a firm of solicitors, but having been 'bitten' by a small firm, I decided to use the biggest firm I could find, even if this meant a trip to the big city. The policy seemed to pay off, for I was soon dealing with a smart, young lady solicitor, who, although requiring much exhortation to do so, prosecuted our adversary to a standstill over the next eighteen months. Before our enemy was vanquished, however, I joined in one of Chris's sessions with the prayer group, where I was left in no doubt that the LORD wished me to forgive my adversary face to face for the pain he had, and was still inflicting on us. A meeting was duly arranged, and I proffered my forgiveness together with a proposed four figure settlement of the claim, only to be met with his uncomprehending gaze and an outright refusal to compromise. The episode had been an early one amongst many during these post conversion years, an exercise in humility, and of going the 'extra mile' in the face of a dogged hostility that showed no pity.

The Regime

Throughout this embattled time, Chris remained as thoroughly anorexic in behavior as ever, and was once again nearing a life-threatening five stones in weight. In the early summer, a serious asthma attack had resulted in an emergency, 'middle-of-the-night,' admission to hospital, requiring a stay of a few days in order to stabilize her condition. It was abundantly clear to the emergency doctor that he was dealing with a very emaciated lady, whose medical history of self-harm gave cause for concern, and when Chris was told he was consulting a psychiatrist colleague, she quickly discharged herself. Before doing so, however, she was able to observe a curious phenomenon, across those few days of recuperation spent in a medical ward.

The great danger with asthma is the increased strain on the heart, and this was of special concern given Chris's advanced anorexic condition, so much so, that her heart was monitored remotely. Information would be transmitted to the 'cardiac room,' whose staff were able to alert the ward supervisor by telephone, in the event of an emergency. As she lay there 'hooked up' to the cardiac room, Chris would often pray, and as she did so, she found that this invariably brought the nurses rushing to her bedside to check on her condition. In all, this must have occurred some five or six times, leading to the seemingly inescapable conclusion, that her bodily functions of heart rate and blood pressure were being affected by her prayers. Clearly, this wouldn't be the first time that the Holy Spirit's attendance in response to prayer has had physiological consequences, with the first recorded incident occurring at Pentecost to the 'drunken disciples' (Acts 2:13,15).

On her return home, Chris simply carried on where she left off, with her daily food intake amounting to little more than two rounds of burnt toast and a banana. It wasn't the quantity of Chris's food intake, however, that impressed itself upon one of her friends from college days, but was instead the erratic nature of her meals, which seemed to hold the key to a remedy. Our 'angelic' friend felt this so strongly, that she offered to spend a two week holiday with Chris, regularising that food regime. Chris's friend, Sheila, was an avid bird watcher and animal enthusiast, and so it seemed ideal that the two of them should holiday in a nearby valley, renowned for its wildlife. I was able to rent a farm cottage for them at the heart of this partially wooded valley, and whilst I continued to work from home, they would spend the days driving the country lanes and watching the foxes, deer, and herons. We quickly established a routine, and most evenings I would travel the four miles or so to the cottage, after which we would all pop over to the local pub for a drink. But it was during the daytime that most headway was made, as Sheila—a very forceful character—imposed a routine upon the day, ensuring that Chris rose for breakfast *time*, before they left to buy a paper, to shop or perhaps watch the heron fish. Lunch*time* was equally regularized, and could either be spent in the local pub or back at the cottage, before an afternoon's activities of various kinds soon brought tea*time*. It was a very exhausting regimen for Chris, who, even with Sheila's gentle persuasion, was still consuming less than five hundred calories per day, every one of which she counted. Nevertheless, the training worked and at the end of two weeks Sheila was exhorting me to maintain the regime she had begun. Strangely, Chris cooperated in all this, and it seemed puzzling until I realized that the very regularity permitted her to calculate her intake all the more accurately. In order to maintain Chris's cooperation, I acquiesced when she requested elaborate salads comprised of fresh herbs, sesame seeds, and celery, knowing all the time that these meals were nutritionally almost valueless. The regime of three, not quite 'square' meals a day, was maintained however, and we began to use our much neglected dining room—the most pleasant, indeed the cosiest room in the house—to take 'time out' to enjoy our meals together. This re-introduction of the social element to meal times was perhaps the most significant feature of the new regime.

5

Body Language

THE WEATHER DURING THE cottage holiday had been particularly cool with a considerable amount of rain, but in August it began to improve. At least it became warmer, so much so, that by the middle of the month the nights had become hot, sticky, and sultry affairs, and it was on airless nights such as these, that Chris tended to have asthma attacks. One Sunday morning in particular stands out, when Chris, suffering from yet another chest infection and breathless from the night before, felt unable to join our son, Stuart, and I at church. It didn't seem to be an especially bad attack, and seemed well capable of control by judicious use of the Ventolin inhaler kept at the bedside. Having been sufficiently reassured by Chris, we were both sent off to church, while she returned to bed for the remainder of the morning. Before very long, however, Chris found herself in the throes of an extremely serious and very severe asthma attack—her own diarized words describe the events as they unfolded:

> I suddenly found myself alone, having a severe attack. I followed my usual routine in such circumstances, using firstly my inhaler and then the nebulizer, which was on loan from the doctor, but nothing was working. The peak flow meter had fallen to fifty (in normal breathing, the breath peak-flows at four hundred!), and my pulse was so rapid I couldn't count it. I felt violently sick, but knew I mustn't be because I didn't have the breath—I

would simply choke. Darkness started to close in on me, and I thought, this is it, the end, in the next few minutes my struggle will be over, there's nothing more I can do, no one to help, too late even for an ambulance—not that I could get downstairs to the 'phone. Then a realisation hit me—the thought, you can turn to God, came to me.

So having had this revelation—if you like, I began to pray. I said, "well Father, it's up to you now, I can't do anything, and there's no one else to help. It's just me and you. Tell me what to do, tell me what I should pray." Then wham, it was there, just a sentence, so I spoke it out loud as best I could, but nothing happened. Then another sentence, so I added that—out loud. Still nothing, it was getting darker. I prayed again saying out loud, "I choose life, I don't want to die anymore," then another sentence came and I said all three out loud, over and over, until I ran out of breath. I carried on saying them over again in my mind, slowly shaking my head to try and emphasize my defiance of death. Then it happened—I felt like someone had wrapped me in a warm blanket, I felt this wonderful warmth spread through my body and my heart rate began to slow. The burning in my chest slowly eased, my breathing became less difficult and the darkness began to recede.

In church that morning, the spot normally reserved for the sermon was given over to a guest speaker, who gave his personal testimony, recounting how he had been wrongly convicted of murder, and his seven year fight to prove his innocence. During his imprisonment, he had come to Christ, and this had resulted in his receipt of considerable spiritual gifts, including what was known in charismatic circles as 'the gift of knowledge.' This was demonstrated, when, after relating his story, he led the church in a time of ministry, and prayed with people individually. Some minutes into the ministry time, he announced that he needed to pray with someone present who was concerned for his mother's health, and Stuart knew that this message was intended for him. Now it could be argued that this was hardly a convincing demonstration of a 'supernatural' gifting, but it was soon validated in what followed.

Stuart responded reluctantly to the (inner) call to go down to the front of the packed church because he was embarrassed, but he did go down and was duly prayed with by the speaker. As they prayed together for Chris, Stuart remembers that he felt unexplained warmth spreading through his body, whilst I too felt similar unexplained warmth spreading throughout my own body, as I looked on from the balcony. Our return home found

Chris in much better shape than when we had left her; indeed she was almost euphoric as she recounted the events of the morning. When she had finished her tale we told her our own story, and on comparing notes, we discovered that Chris's escape from the 'gates of death' had taken place at precisely three minutes past twelve—the same time as our own 'warming!' In her diary record in the weeks following this time, Chris also records how she felt that the Sunday morning asthma attack had been the devil's work, mounted to prevent her survival. It might be argued that in holding this view, Chris had been influenced by a common tendency among some charismatic Christians, to overly personify the spiritual content of a 'lucky' recovery from what should be viewed simply as a medical crisis. There is, however, a full description in scripture of a similar situation to the one Chris experienced, a description, which is eminently more satisfying than a first or literal reading of this text might suggest.

The text in question is the central prayer of the second chapter of Jonah, which begins with Jonah 1:17—a verse which is only found separated from chapter 2 in English translations of the bible. Indeed, the 'swallowing' of Jonah may be seen to mark the beginning of an oppression, similar to Saul's experience in 1 Samuel 16:14, and within which he is trapped and powerless. In addition to noting her own powerlessness, Chris's account records a stubborn, self-reliance which acts as a bar to a much more intimate (saving) relationship with God. Jonah commences his prayer from the belly (Greek, *koilia*) of the fish, and this term appears in each of the first three verses of chapter 2 in the Greek (LXX) text, and carries the meaning of 'the deepest insides.' The increasingly progressive darkness related in Chris's account mirrors Jonah's descent into increasing blackness, as he moves from dark ship's hold to darker sea bed, to be then followed by his incarceration in the oppressor's (fish's) innards, the darkest place of all. Jonah's imprisonment leads eventually to his remembrance of the LORD, and his prayer summarized in verse seven was replicated exactly by Chris in her own moment of greatest need. Thus, in reality, these events did not occur in the belly of a (literal) fish; they happened inside Jonah himself, and record the transition from one level of relationship with God, to a more intimate, reliant, and indeed saving relationship with him. Chris had followed Jonah's example, forging an intimate, relationship with God in a situation where no other help was forthcoming. In her diary record, Chris writes: "I'd asked, I'd listened, I'd followed his instructions, and I came back from the 'gates of death' with a *completely new understanding and relationship* with God."

"Hold My Hand"

The crisis of that Sunday morning in the middle of August had taken place some four months after Chris's commitment, and that time had been packed with some very strange phenomena indeed. In fact, strange things began to occur soon after I had 'come out' as a Christian, that is, as soon as I had revealed my own Christian commitment to Chris, and just after she began to be involved with the prayer group. It all seemed to stem from a private prayer of my own (our prayers remained mostly private for quite a long time), in which I had asked the LORD to 'hold my hand,' and which was—I thought—a fairly innocuous allusion to my great need for help with our legal and financial problems. Immediately after that prayer, however, I began to notice some strange sensations in my hands whenever we prayed together. In particular, I found these feelings to be coincident with questions—or more to the point—answers to questions we were praying. Whenever we identified a positive answer to prayer—often later, and/or through other more 'conventional' means, we were able to associate this with a sensation in the nerve endings of the palms of my hands. It seemed to be a kind of simple binary code, where the 'o' or absence of sensation indicated a negative answer, and where the '1' was the presence of tingling, buzzing feelings in my hands, indicating a positive response.

Despite diligent searches in the later years of my theological training, I was never able to find much in the way of scriptural validation for this phenomenon, save to say that the basic principle of questioning by lot is a well-established device for questioning the LORD, found in the Old Testament. Indeed, the Urim and Thummim first noted in Exodus 28:30 seems to have been such a device, which the priests used for determining the divine will, in matters where a choice of two alternatives was posed. Moreover, it would seem quite logical, that the basic principle of questioning the LORD had not ceased with the giving of the Holy Spirit at Pentecost, but that the Means of Response might simply be more immediately to hand! Eventually, over a number of years, one grows to trust these sensations, but at the outset I remained rather sceptical, even though these feelings were happening to me, indeed, were within my own body. Although we later came to know a prominent elder of a large, local church, who also experienced similar phenomena, at the time we simply had no means of 'objectively'—and I use the word advisedly—evaluating what was happening.

Madness

Right from the early days of my commitment to the LORD, I had decided that He had to perform—He simply had to 'do the business!' I certainly wasn't interested in a god who couldn't outperform the efforts of 'enlightened' scientific man, who couldn't interact with the physical world—including human bodies, or who couldn't directly influence (not overrule) the minds of believer and unbeliever alike. But these sensations were something else, and in those first weeks and months I began to wonder whether they were a figment of my imagination. The prayer group were very understanding, and were quite willing to accept that the manifestations of the Holy Spirit were many and varied, yet they had no direct experience of others who had such a personal, 'dialogical' relationship with the LORD. Finally, my doubts became so intense, that I was compelled to test (Him on) these phenomena, and so we prayed together to do just that. Our prayer 'stance' had—at least following our connection with the prayer group—been one of either sitting or standing with the palms of the hands held open facing upwards. This was a typically 'charismatic' attitude of prayer usually accompanied by keeping the eyes open, and on that particular day I was stood leaning against the Rayburn cooker for warmth. It was Chris who prayed, *silently* requesting a validation of these feelings. The response was immediate, and I felt a rush from both my arms into my hands, of what has sadly, for want of a more accurate word, to be described as 'tingling.' Words always seem to fail to convey an understanding of what is felt, if only because the sensations differ slightly each time. Sometimes, the feeling is simply a tingling, but on other occasions there are vibrations, or a strange heaviness in the hands—as if they were suddenly filled with something. Quite early on, I came to recognize that a sensation in the thumb would indicate a positive response—most frequently of positive reassurance, and this particular 'thumbs up' feeling could be so intense that the thumb would lock up rigid. Indeed, there was one occasion at a bible week some years later, when I was feeling especially miserable, feeling excluded, and unable to join in with the 'happy clappy,' full-of-joy (what's that?), dancing Christians. We were camping, and had got into our sleeping bags, having left the worship time early. As I mulled over the unhappy events of the evening, I asked in silent prayer, whether I was really in relationship with Him, given that I seemed unable to join in with what, at times, seemed learned and hysterical behavior? At that moment I received the usual 'thumbs up,' this time, however, not only did my thumb lock rigid, but also my entire forearm did likewise. I guess it was important for me to know the extent of my acceptance! Looking back, that early test was probably the point at which the emphasis in our prayer life first began to change from private, individual prayer to prayer in corporate union, albeit a union of just the two of us.

"Buzzes," "Lifts" and "Creeps"

Thumbs are interesting things, they hurt like hell and bleed profusely when cut, because they carry a large blood vessel, and this prevents them being used to take a pulse. When a pulse is taken, it would be easier and more natural to use the thumb, but because the thumb contains its own pulse, the fingers are used instead to avoid confusion when the beats are being counted. A strong pulse in the thumb was one of the more unusual sensations I experienced during these early prayer times, and the pulse would almost always come in response to a particular prayer, last a few seconds, and then cease. It could have been easily explained if my heart rate had been high at these times, but prayer is of its essence a quiet, sedentary activity, during which the heart is in perhaps its most tranquil state. The sensation of a pulse in my thumb in response to prayer, would we discovered, indicate rather more than the simple positive affirmation of a 'thumbs up,' and the feeling would usually signify that the topic of the prayer was close to the LORD's heart.

We spent a great deal of time in those early weeks and months enthusiastically trying to codify all the various 'buzzes' and 'lifts' which we both experienced. With the benefit of hindsight, I suspect that all of the elaborate system we developed was exactly that—an elaborate *human* system, which is not to say that it wasn't utilized or rather 'honored' by the LORD to aid in his desire to communicate with us. Authorities within both the church and academia acknowledge that it is the desire of God to speak to his people, but few elaborate on how this is to be achieved twenty centuries on from the Christ event. The salient point for us, however, was the very fact of these sensations, which came in response to prayer, giving us the everyday, point by point guidance we sought. Perhaps such a communication 'system' could only be developed in our particular circumstances, that is, where two people—the minimum number required for corporate prayer—had the time available for such experimentation. Because I now worked at home, I was only two flights of stairs away from Chris, and hence was immediately available for such activity—at least, during our now regularized mealtimes.

Although our attempted systematisation of the sensations was largely a failure, several have continued to remain useful adjuncts to other, later modes of communication. In addition to the 'thumbs up'—both with and without pulse—already mentioned, there was a similar feeling in the index finger, a kind of brief, itchy tickle indicating that the LORD was either stressing, or pointing something out. Much later on, fully a year later in fact, Chris developed what she came to call her 'creep'. The 'creep' was by far the most bizarre of these sensations, consisting of a strong tickle on the shoulder blade, which Chris likened to the sensation produced when an insect crawls over the skin. It was always in the same spot and had an intensity that was almost beyond endurance, in order, we later concluded, to grab her attention. The attention grabbing nature of this sensation made it quite unique, insofar as it was not merely a bidden response of prayer, rather, it often came as a confirmation of a *thought*, that *either one* of us were having at the time. As often as not, however, Chris would only realize she was being 'creeped' belatedly, whereupon we would both have to try to recollect our past half dozen thoughts, which is not the easiest of tasks. But then, as the correct thought was brought back to mind, she would be 'creeped' again in confirmation!

The Exorcism

It might be argued that the sensations in my hands, codified or otherwise, were of little use to others and as such did little to enhance or promote the glory of God. Countering this analysis would be difficult, if it were not for one particular incident during which the sensations were put to good use, in wider group prayer. The incident involved a young lady, then in her early twenties, who had come to the attention of the prayer group via a mutual friend. Although a Christian herself, she had been troubled by bizarre problems at home—a fairly 'well heeled' home—for fully nine years, and things had now come to a head. It turned out that she was experiencing pronounced supernatural activity on a nightly basis, during which objects were hurled across the bedroom, doors banged violently shut and her bible thrown face down on the floor. Things had come to such a pass that her minister had been exhorted to visit the house in an attempt to 'cleanse It.' Sadly, his visit proved unsuccessful and the young lady's friend—a fellow member of our own church—mentioned her plight to the prayer group in desperation.

Our first sight of this lady, as we welcomed her to our home, clearly indicated that all was not well. Indeed, the person standing before us could only be described as disheveled, with red puffy eyes peering out from under unkempt hair, and it was quite clear that she had gone without sleep for some days past. In all, there were six of us there that morning, for in addition to our 'subject', those present included two prayer group members plus ourselves, along with the young lady's friend. The group prayer session that then unfolded was truly remarkable, and revealed the awful background to the supernatural manifestations. For the better part of an hour the assembled group prayed, to reveal that our guest's parental home had been built on an ancient pagan worship site, for what had once been a wooded hill was now a small, country estate of expensive detached houses. Ba'al worship, or its early Britannic equivalent, was the root cause of our friend's problem, or more particularly, the demonic forces lying at the heart of such worship.

With open bibles and making full use of my 'sensations,' we were able to discern that the nocturnal disturbances resulted from an unholy alliance between the demonic reality behind the ancient pagan worship, and a lesser spirit, both of whom were still linked to this physical location. It was then a relatively simple matter of exercising our Christian authority over such powers, that is, by binding and expelling them from the house. We had no more dealings with the young lady after that time, except for the receipt of a thank-you letter affirming the efficacy of the action taken. Much later on, however, we were to come across our friend, who had by then become a vibrant and vivacious participating member of another Christian congregation, showing no sign whatsoever of her erstwhile problem. This was the only exorcism we were ever to be involved in, and it was remarkably atypical in that it was achieved fully three miles distant from the afflicted site.

The Potential for Misinterpretation

In considered hindsight, some of our early attempts to codify or systematize the bodily sensations, were probably a bad mistake, especially given the fact that we still mostly prayed alone, coming together only to question the LORD. As a consequence, the development and maintenance of a healthy scepticism concerning even that, which was received when praying together, is the lasting outcome of this period. At the time, however, we failed to test the responses given in a thorough enough manner, often making unjustified assumptions, on the basis of what was, at best, merely a choice between alternatives. Gradually, over a period of some months we developed the rule of never going beyond the information given, and this stood us in good stead, when later on, more sophisticated means of communication were added to these responses. Listening to God is an activity which always carries with it the potential for misinterpretation, and in our experience this potential seems to be at its highest during individual, or private prayer. Group engagement in listening prayer significantly reduces this risk, even where the 'group' in question amounts to no more than two people!

Listening to God is an activity that is encouraged within the church, but it is not really considered 'proper' to question or 'inquire of the LORD' as so many Old Testament characters did, from Rebekah onwards (Gen. 25:22). Most divinatory enquiry found in the Old Testament is by individuals who are frequently prophets (1 Kings 22:7,8), but there is also a limited precedent and mandate for group divinatory enquiry (1 Sam. 10:5,10). In these latter verses prophecy appears to be a corporate activity, which is extended, or 'democratized' in a manner of speaking, in the New Testament when the Holy Spirit or Spirit of Prophecy is given to 'all flesh' (Acts 2:17; cf Joel 2:28). As a consequence, a much larger group of potential prophets became possible. With this expansion of the prophetic franchise, the possibilities for error within the divine experience might also have multiplied, perhaps leading to Paul's insistence on good order at Corinth, and his exhortation to persist with prophecy at Thessalonika. Indeed, the major problem with the Thessalonian church may have been a perception that prophecy was failing to resolve their eschatological concerns, that is, they were worried and concerned about precisely when the risen Jesus would return (1 Thess. 5). Paul's exhortations to both churches, are therefore, concerned with the adoption of appropriate procedures to effect error-free prophecy. Moreover, Paul submits his own words of advice to testing by the same process of responsory prayer-dialogue (1 Cor. 14:37; 1 Thess. 5:4). Despite the capacity for error and misinterpretation having been increased significantly with the giving of the Spirit at Pentecost, the means of eradicating error was, and is, the self-same corporate nature of group listening prayer.

6

Healings

THE HEALING PRAYER GROUP'S work with Chris through the summer and autumn of 1992 was, as has been noted, heavily influenced by the then current charismatic climate of the Wimber/Vineyard movement. As also noted, the group was comprised of four women, two of whom were the mothers of small children who often accompanied them to morning prayer sessions, and who almost always played quietly on the floor whilst their mums prayed. A third member of the group was the mother of older children, and although the wife of a highly paid professional was nearing the point of resuming an active and creative professional career of her own. The fourth member was an older lady who belonged to the lay leadership of our new church, and whose major occupation consisted of caring for a family member. Apart from their readings of the popular charismatic books and articles of the time, none of them had any training, qualifications or expertise in anything which even closely resembled counselling work. Indeed, in terms of past training and qualifications, they had between them three first degrees, two of which were science degrees, Chemistry and Physics in particular, and certainly nothing which the world would recognize as fitting them for counselling the suicidally depressed.

Again, as related earlier, Chris was in regular contact with professional social workers, who met with her for perhaps an hour twice weekly, as a part of the 'early warning' monitoring of her anorexia and depression. During these sessions, it would be natural for Chris to be engaged in counselling, or more accurately, cognitive-behavioral therapy, in an attempt to alter her perceptions of, and attitudes to her deep-seated problems. Remarkably, it soon became apparent during the meetings with social workers, that the issues raised during professional therapy, had already been raised and dealt with, in a prayer group session the previous day. It seemed that Chris's deep psychological hurts were being infallibly raised and addressed *during* prayer with the group, rendering the subsequent cognitive-behavioral therapy redundant. It was the social worker herself who first noticed this pattern, wherein a group of untrained, middle-class housewives were unerringly pre-empting the outcomes of the latest psychology based therapy. The parallel between the prayer group's work and that of the social workers became particularly pronounced during the autumn, when Chris underwent a period of great psychological stress, in the immediate aftermath of her first healing.

Anorexia and Self-Hatred

In her struggle with death on that August Sunday morning, Chris's determination to seek the LORD's help had been underpinned by her experience of the previous two or three weeks. Throughout this time, she had had engendered within her a growing excitement and anticipation, that something good was going to happen to her, which would be of life-changing significance. This build up of 'unknowing' anticipation had begun to point to, and centre upon, the morning meeting with the prayer group on the following Wednesday. The arrival of the chest infection that weekend had heralded a difficult time ahead, and even when the Sunday morning asthma crisis had passed, Chris remained in the throes of the infection for some days. I became sufficiently concerned across the Sunday night, to decide to involve the doctor, and duly did so early on the Monday morning. Chris knew that a visit from the doctor might well result in hospitalisation, but reluctantly agreed—at my insistence—to see her. Both Chris and I knew what to expect in these circumstances, and when the doctor arrived, we were unsurprised as she fired off her full and well tried armoury of yet stronger antibiotics (for the infection) and Ventolin nebules for the asthma. The doctor, who was a very meek and mild person, 'demanded' that she be allowed to remove Chris to hospital, but she was easily overcome by a Chris who was determined to pray with the prayer group on Wednesday morning, leaving the doctor with little recourse, save to return the following day. Tuesday duly arrived and found Chris still in some distress with her breathing, and continuing to resist hospitalisation, quipping to the doctor that the peak-flow reading of 100 was "one of her better days." Unable to get Chris to cooperate, the doctor prescribed oral steroids, in place of the steroids which the hospital would have given by injection, and left promising to return again the next day.

The prayer group met at ten o'clock on Wednesday morning minus two members, and after inviting the Holy Spirit to participate, the session began with an initial prayer asking the LORD what He wanted them to pray for. In its practice, prayer ministry is a process or sequence of sessions with the client, which always involve the invocation of the Holy Spirit, and thereby, the seeking of God's guidance. What is always remarkable about such sessions, is the difference between the needs of the client as perceived beforehand, and the actual agenda addressed by God. Indeed, as Leanne Payne observes, "the sicknesses of spirit, soul and body intertwine and overlap. It is not at all unusual to pray for the healing of a memory and see the body healed as well." Thus, prayer ministry is essentially a process punctuated by revelations from God, whereby *He* addresses and prioritizes the problems in the client's life. The observation by the social workers involved with Chris, that sophisticated psychotherapy was being undertaken during these sessions, indicates that the Christian counsellor is singularly placed to minister through prayer, to the sick person, who can be treated as an integral whole. This is possible because the Christian 'psychotherapist' has access to an overall view of man which is not a human perspective, but rather, it is divine in origin and he/she is consequently able to apply that insight to the healing process.

On this occasion, one of the group, Pat, had brought with her a book she had mentioned to Chris during the previous week, and all three of them were agreed, that it 'felt right' that Chris should pray one particular prayer from this book. The book in question was Leanne Payne's "Restoring the Christian Soul—Through Healing Prayer," and the prayer Chris read out from it was entitled 'the renunciation of self-hatred.' Although still suffering from breathlessness, Chris was able to pray the long prayer renouncing her self-hatred, and later notes in her diary, that she didn't feel particularly different afterwards. Indeed, all the anticipation that this was the final step to 'physical' healing seemed to have been mere wishful thinking, for "there were no great bolts of lightening," and the only benefit seemed to be a very slight easing of her breathing. Exhausted by the session, Chris returned to bed after her friends had left and began to meditate as she often did on such occasions. Meditation techniques had been offered to Chris as occupational therapy during her incarcerations in hospital, and the subsequent visits to the Day Care Centre. Following her Christian commitment, Chris began to superimpose Christian themes on her meditations, replacing the secular concepts and ideas that had originally been introduced to her. During this particular meditation, Chris felt that the LORD wished me to pray through that same prayer—the renunciation of self-hatred—and became convinced of the need for this across that afternoon.

It was about four o'clock when Chris broached the subject, after I had finished working in the upstairs office, and not being completely *au fait* with the earlier goings-on, I felt the very idea was ludicrous in the extreme. Now I could well understand how someone suffering from anorexia nervosa—with all its attendant distortions of perceived self worth—might hate themselves, but how I wondered, could such self-hatred possibly apply to me? Nevertheless, I acceded to her request and we prayed the same prayer together, and as I sat by the bed, the most remarkable experience ensued. Coming into a situation of prayer from a worldly business environment, could not possibly have prepared me for what happened next, for I found myself caught up inside a kind of daytime vision. As I spoke the words of the prayer out loud, I 'felt' myself physically lifted up before a figure of the crucified Jesus, looking at his face as He hung there. What happened next took me completely by surprise, for I—an introverted Englishman not given to kissing anyone—found myself kissing this face on each cheek in turn, an action that I did with some revulsion. I was repulsed by the *blackness* of His face, a blackness, which was not that of normal skin pigmentation, but rather the blackness of deep bruising—all over, and through and through. Whether I renounced self-hatred in my deepest *psyche* that day remains a moot point, but I will never forget that vision of Jesus.

This interlude must have lasted perhaps half an hour, and afterwards Chris got up and left to keep an appointment with her social worker, firstly ensuring that she took a sufficient number of 'puffs' of her Ventolin to 'get her through.' On her return she decided to go back to bed, if only to use the nebulizer, since she was again breathless. Following a brief discussion about the evening meal with Stuart, she left the kitchen, picking up an apple from the fruit bowl as she did so. After nebulising, Chris's breathing eased sufficiently to allow her to concentrate on doing the newspaper crossword, as she awaited the evening meal, and as she did this, she ate the apple. It was fully ten minutes after eating the apple that the uncharacteristically bizarre nature of this simple act—eating an apple—impressed itself on Chris's mind. The following series of thoughts—recorded in her diary—illustrate the momentous significance of this act for an anorexic:

> "I've just eaten that apple. I don't believe it"!
> "I've just eaten an apple whilst waiting for a meal. I can't eat food which is extra to my requirements"!

"I didn't circle the fruit bowl for half an hour, until I had plucked up the courage to take it"!
"I didn't sit looking at it for an hour, trying to talk myself into eating it"!
"I didn't feel it go down"!
"I didn't want to get rid of it. I wasn't panic struck"!
"I didn't want to rip myself open and take it out again."

Gradually, beginning with this seemingly insignificant 'snack' (the very concept of a 'snack' is alien to anorexics!), the awesome effects of that healing prayer became apparent over succeeding days. Indeed, the full import became clear on the very next day, when Chris ran out of dog food whilst attempting to feed our two young dogs. In desperation she located a tin of spicy bean soup—the chunky variety—and made up their meals with some of it, whilst thinking to herself "that looks nice." Whilst still reeling from the realisation that she had expressed desire for food, the thought was quickly followed by the decision to try the remaining half tin of the soup for her meal that evening. Chris knew the calorific content of every food there was, and the fact that this soup was a 'chunky' soup—full of beans and potatoes—did not trigger the usual anorexic reaction of revulsion in her. When I came home that evening from visiting clients, I asked Chris what she wanted to eat, and I apparently did this in a resigned, 'this is going to be hard work,' kind of voice. Imagine my surprise at being told she would try the soup! This delight must have registered on my face, to the extent that my mouth dropped open, remaining so, as Chris asked for accompanying bread and a sweet to follow! The tinned soup tasted "awful, just like every other tinned soup," Chris confided to her diary, but after she had eaten this meal, she didn't have the usual anorexic panic attack. It was at this point that she believed that things had changed for good.

'Spiritual Healings'—Past Hurts

In the weeks that followed it certainly seemed as if the central psychological or 'spiritual' core of Chris's anorexia had been addressed and dealt with, but had it? The renunciation of self-hatred was it turned out the 'tip of the iceberg,' or to use another analogy, it had opened a Pandora's box of further problems, all revolving around Chris's estimation of her own self-worth. Across the autumn and through the winter of 92/3 the prayer group continued to minister to Chris in a number of areas, as her weight hovered at the low end of the six to seven stone range, but stayed above lower life-threatening levels. Although we didn't know it at the time, the anorexia was beaten, and increasingly the social worker's reports began to show the predominance of another problem, that of chronic or resistive depression. The diary entries of the autumn meetings with the prayer group record the return of the anger, low mood, agitation, and suicidal intent, after the brief summer interlude of relative euphoria. Throughout this period, the prayer group were instrumental in the discernment and expulsion of spirits, which have been regarded within psychiatry as disintegrated psychological components of the person him(her)self. Indeed, during one of the sessions, Chris had a picture in which she saw herself standing beside and outside herself—two persons in fact—black and white, good and evil. The remedial prayer applied to this situation was one in which Chris forgave her other self, and in so doing, effected a re-integration, whilst at the same time 'expelling' the bad characteristics. Immediately after having prayed this prayer, Chris describes feeling as if "a great weight had been lifted off her," and of a "black cloud having been dispersed."

Less than a week later the situation was scarcely improved, with Chris's diary entry again recording very low mood, and indeed, the prayer sessions of that October began to reveal that Chris's past hurts were intimately entwined with this depression. Prayer sessions which began with her expressed feelings of agitation, anger, and suicidal intent often revealed past traumas, such as two attempted rapes and one instance of child sexual abuse, before she became assuaged by the LORD's peace. Past problems such as these had engendered issues of self-worth—one of the DSM IV ("Diagnostic and Statistical Manual of Mental Disorders") criteria for a major depressive episode—that ultimately led to the questioning of her very identity, including questions about why a person should love or live at all. Just like Chris, Jonah's anger (Jon. 4:1, 4, 9) was also symptomatic of depression, which is to be seen as one of the most common masking operations for deep seated personal anxiety. The similarity between Chris and Jonah does not end there, however, for both displayed 'suicidality,' or more accurately "recurrent thoughts of death," (Jon. 4:8–9) which is another, significant attribute of a major depression episode found in the DSM IV criteria. I have argued elsewhere that these features (anger and 'suicidality') of Jonah's discourse with the LORD take place within an altered state of consciousness—a dream, which because of its length and position within a normal night's sleep is also *characteristic* of depression. Indeed, Hobson is clear that "major depression . . . is a functional disorder of the very same neuronal systems that control dreaming;" and goes on to suggest that "to be prone to depression is to be prone to REM sleep (dreaming) and vice versa." Anti-depressant drugs interfere with the display of patterns of dreaming that are characteristic of depression, and as a result these did not feature in Chris's experience of the condition. Chris was able, with the prayer group's assistance, to forgive those who had sinned against her in the past, but unfortunately, although helpful in itself, the cancellation of past sins did not address Chris's problems of self-worth, since she continued to feel that she was in some way responsible for those events. The restoration of her self-worth, and the reconstruction and maintenance of a new, guilt free identity, then became the object of this process of prayer therapy over the next twelve months.

Compassion

Although the summer had brought with it inroads into Chris's 'mental' illnesses, there had been little, if any, healing of the physical aspects of the chronic fatigue syndrome. Indeed, if physical illness can be separated from psychiatric illness or immune and nervous system defects, there had been precious little evidence of physical healing as such. To the sceptical observer it could have seemed, that as new Christians, we were deluding ourselves into believing that real healing had taken place, and that a true physical test of Christian healing had yet to take place. If such a test were needed, it presented itself that autumn, in the form of a physical emergency quite unconnected with Chris's other problems. The sequence of events began with neck pain—at least the pain began in her neck—which slowly began to arch over to her temples across a three day period, becoming both continuous and excruciating until she was finally compelled to visit the doctor. After failing to make a diagnosis, the nonplussed GP suggested Chris sought the help of a private osteopath, thinking that an informed manipulation of Chris's neck joints—once severely whip lashed in a car accident—might solve the problem. The visit to the osteopath left Chris with the loan of a neck brace, and poorer by a twenty five pound fee, but still in pain. On the following day Chris telephoned her friend (who I shall call Pat), and she came to the house with another prayer group member (who I shall call Anne), in order to pray with her. It was during the late morning, when I was doing some office work in the converted attic, that unusually, they called me downstairs to join them in prayer.

Although I agreed to join them I really couldn't see the point, after all, what could four people achieve in prayer that three couldn't? Nevertheless, I joined them out of concern for Chris and sat down on the sofa beside her, whilst Anne knelt on the carpet to her left. Both of us laid hands on Chris, and I prayed silently with my left hand resting on her neck, as Anne prayed for healing and Pat prayed in tongues. As I sat there I began to feel uncomfortable, and at first I attributed this to my waistcoat (I wore three piece suits for business in those days), which was a good fit. But the strange feeling that began in my lower abdomen, far from subsiding, began to build up. The feeling was one of swirling, boiling seething fluidity, which began to move up my body causing a film of sweat to break out on the brow of my head, as it continued to build up. Eventually, the swirling, boiling motion, together with the heat, became so intense that I felt sure I would pass out. Finally, the whole 'thing,' which was now in my neck and shoulders, spurted at great speed down my left arm, which still rested on Chris's neck. Pat and Anne on hearing my bewildered account of this phenomenon, immediately labelled it as a manifestation of the Holy Spirit, expecting Chris to announce she was now free of pain. The pain remained, however, but from that point on began to diminish, and over the next twelve hours it receded in exactly the opposite way to the way in which it had arrived—disappearing from her temples towards her neck. Throughout this time, the fast decreasing pain was accompanied by a discharge down the back of Chris's throat, indicating that something—perhaps an abscess—had burst. It wasn't until much later on, during my theological studies in fact, that I discovered the exact nature of that strange and uncomfortable manifestation of the Holy Spirit.

To begin with, I found parallels between my experience that day and the description of the Holy Spirit found in the Young's literal translation of John 7:38:

> he who is believing in me, according as the Writing said, Rivers
> out of his belly shall flow of living water.

The first thing I noted was the similarity between what I had felt—the swirling, eddying spurting motions—and the rivers or streams of water, which are described as living, not least, because of their motion or quickness. Moreover, there is also the similarity between the energetic waters described more fully by Jesus to the woman at the well (John 4:10), and the actual well water. The well is almost certainly fed by a spring bubbling up out of the rock deep below, and the woman continues to think that Jesus is referring to this physical spring. The word used for spring in the Greek is *pege*, which significantly, can also be used to describe a fountain or a hemorrhage of blood, and these analogies convey precisely the spurting action of the Holy Spirit, that is intended here. Secondly, Jesus' analogy carries a resonance between spurting *blood* and *living water*, and the intention may be to convey a sense of the felt warmth of the Spirit likened to warm-blooded, mammalian/human life. Finally, there is the origin of the Holy Spirit—deep in the belly (Gk. *koilia*) or abdomen, just as the spring bubbles up from deep within the rock—the belly of the earth.

Interestingly, Paul, when describing God's love in Romans 5:5 also uses a verb (Greek—*ekcheo*), which can refer to the shedding of blood, as with the KJV translation:

> And hope maketh not ashamed; because the love of God is shed abroad in our hearts by the Holy Ghost which is given unto us.

What later translations have lost is that factor which unified the cultures of both early seventeenth century England, and the Roman world of the New Testament, namely, armor bearing soldiers. Battle for both involved aiming a sword blow at the space between armored shoulder and helmeted head, that is, at the neck, and a successfully administered blow would result in blood *spurting* from the severed jugular artery. It is this spurting action that is to be experienced inside our hearts, or more properly, deep inside our *cores* (heart—Latin *cordibus*), and by means of the Holy Spirit. Paul's use of this verb also signifies his Jewish understanding that the life of anything, whether animal or human, resides in the blood, and indicates an experiential understanding that love and life are functions of, and personified in, the Holy Spirit.

The spurting action that I experienced had direction, indeed it traveled from me to Chris down my left arm, as it rested on her neck, and later prompted me to ask, what, if anything, does the bible have to say about this? Such a transfer is described in at least one place—Mark 5:30, which reads in the NRSV version:

> Immediately aware that power had gone forth from him, Jesus turned about in the crowd and said, "Who touched my clothes"?

The word translated here as 'power' (Greek, *dynamis*) is used many times in the New Testament, often in connection with healing, and is the word from which the English word 'dynamic' derives. In modern, colloquial English, if a person is described as 'dynamic,' it usually means that the person is regarded as being 'full of life.' Moreover, our scientific use of the word—originating as it does from the physics of the seventeenth and eighteenth centuries—almost always refers to *motion* of some kind or other. Indeed earlier versions of the Anglican creed used to include the words, 'the *quick* and the dead'—the word 'quick' being a synonym for living.

In the ensuing years since Chris's healing that morning, I came to understand that I had experienced exactly the same phenomenon as that undergone by the great Healer, Jesus, the only difference being that it was a once only event for me. I did, however, notice that at least one contemporary, modern 'healer' was familiar with the Holy Spirit in 'healing mode.' John Wimber when speaking about that same passage in Mark 5, records that he had felt something like Jesus' experience, several hundred times during his long, healing-prayer ministry. But why did it happen to me if, unlike Wimber, I wasn't gifted as a 'healer?' Two reasons suggest themselves. Firstly, the pain Chris was undergoing could have had a significantly more serious, and perhaps life-threatening cause, than any of us could know, therefore needing prompt action. Secondly, it might have simply been the LORD's action, in His compassion for the child who was in pain.

7

Hearing Voices?

IN THE AFTERMATH OF the healing from anorexia, and after the summer euphoria had subsided, Chris put on about a stone in weight, bringing her into the six to seven stone range. Chris's weight oscillated in this range throughout the autumn and into the spring of 1993, but although this weight continued to give her social workers cause for concern, it was never again to fall to below six stones. Chronic or resistive depression quickly asserted itself as the major psychiatric problem, manifested as problems of self-worth, which sadly, were reinforced by the actions of the prayer group. Chris's therapy at the hands of the prayer group had resulted in the formation of strong bonds of friendship, and her apparently complete recovery at the end of the summer had led them to include her in regular prayer sessions with other 'clients.' Unfortunately, Chris's weakened condition and ongoing C.F.S. problems meant that she simply didn't have the stamina for such work, because the sessions were so physically and emotionally exhausting. In such circumstances, it was only natural that the group would back away from Chris, in their concern for her welfare. The perception that she was 'not up to the task' would therefore lead Chris into a downward spiral, in which people disengaged from her giving her less responsibility, which, in turn contributed to, and reinforced the downward spiral. It was seemingly a problem that could only be resolved, by replacing the downward spiral with an upward one, one that was self-reinforcing and therefore self-validating.

The trick was to offer Chris reinforcing activities and responsibility, consistent with her health and well being on a daily basis—no easy task!

Practical steps towards initiating this virtuous spiral were agreed between Chris and her social worker, at their December meeting, and were to include formal rest sessions each day, art therapy, medical monitoring at the local health centre and an agreed eating programme. The emphasis lay on ensuring that Chris was well enough to successfully undertake limited activity, and so spiral upwards, because she felt herself to be of value. At a review meeting four months later, a significantly more optimistic atmosphere prevailed, with the social worker reporting that Chris had developed a much stronger sense of her own responsibility for finding a way out of her problems. It was anticipated that full recovery for Chris would still take twelve months, or perhaps considerably longer, but it was significant that even this, not entirely cheerful, prognosis should be made at all. Weight problems persisted, however, and although Chris was now in excess of seven stone, she was discouraged by the return of painful menstruation, together with the muscle and joint pain, which had hitherto been strangely suppressed at the lower weights. The appearance of a new phenomenon accompanied Chris's movement towards recovery—that of bingeing—and this was normally precipitated by negative thoughts about the value of recovery, where such renewed physical pain attended that recovery. In order to avoid bingeing, Chris was able to successfully engage in Christian meditation, or seek out the company of a friend, and use these activities to distract herself from the negative thoughts. Throughout, the GP had steadfastly maintained her belief that the problems had been, and remained, mainly psychological, seeing no benefit in referrals for further physical checks. This was important to Chris, if only because any validation of the physical component of her problems would have an affirming effect upon her—an 'objective' verification of all she had been through—but a formal 'diagnosis' of Chronic Fatigue Syndrome lay nearly three years in the future. Despite this fundamental disagreement lying at the base of their relationship, the doctor recognized the importance of a degree of medical supervision, and agreed to continue to 'monitor' Chris on a monthly basis—mainly in order to weigh her.

Communication with God—Psychosis

At the review meeting in April, Chris's social worker and the GP had estimated her weight at "around the seven stone mark," although I had considered her weight to be seven and a half stone. Significantly, my own estimate was vindicated when, at a weighing in the GP's surgery some twelve days later,

Chris's weight was recorded as seven st. seven lbs.. Perhaps more importantly, the doctor's notes record Chris's desire to be a full stone heavier still, and the July entries in the clinical notes show her weight edging towards eight stone. The persistence of suicidal thoughts throughout the summer had, however, caused the social workers sufficient concern to report the matter to the hospital psychiatric department. As a result of their referral, a home visit was made by a consultant psychiatrist, who in his subsequent report talks about Chris *having had* an eating disorder, and expresses his concern for her mental state as the *sequel* to that illness. Moreover, his considered opinion was that Chris was additionally now suffering from a psychotic illness, which manifested itself as the expression of delusional religious ideas which were not necessarily in keeping with the belief system of the family culture. A second domiciliary visit by another consultant psychiatrist took place some two weeks later, during which I was present and in which he confirmed the earlier diagnosis of psychosis. If, because of my absence during his interview, the first consultant could assume that the family did not share Chris's beliefs—thereby demonstrating variance, then the second one was left in no doubt that both I and my son shared Chris's views. In such circumstances, the second psychiatrist could only demonstrate 'psychosis' by including *all three of us* within his diagnosis, and then contrasting our views with what he assumed were the 'normal' views of the remainder of our church's congregation! It would seem that expressing the reality of communication with God and more particularly *His communication back again*, is psychotic behavior in the modern/post modern age, especially where the person concerned is also suicidally depressed. Interestingly, such behavior taking place in the Israel of nearly three thousand years ago was deemed to be prophetic, as was the case with that other half-starved depressive—Elijah.

What is at issue here is philosophy, in particular medical (psychiatric) philosophy, which takes as its yardstick the perceived 'normality' of the behavior of a person's (patient's?) peer group. Unfortunately, Chris's peer group was (arbitrarily) deemed to be the local Baptist congregation, within which prophetic behavior of the 'Elijah kind,' simply does not take place. Indeed, such behavior does not take place within the (Western) Christian Church at all, and has probably not taken place for many centuries—since ancient times in fact. Sadly, medical personnel are, in the main, heirs to Christian 'orthodoxy' in its most reactionary form, in these 'post Christian' times. This is partly the fault of the Church, which following the closure of the Canon, considers any significant revelation from God to be unlikely in the extreme. On the other hand, thinking, committed Christians at the 'grassroots' level would all acknowledge that God still communicates with His people, but that this is usually a contingent, mitigated affair and hardly ever *direct* and *immediate*. The failure of the Church to acknowledge, still less support such prophetic behavior, stems at least in part from an over emphasis on the *oracular* elements of prophecy, at the expense of the *dialogic* dimension. Although the Church would agree that New Testament prophecy was essentially the same as that of the Old Testament, it frequently neglects to include in its portrayal of either, that which is perhaps the most important function of the prophet—his role as God's confidant. Thus, in circumstances where the medical profession classes much aberrant behavior as 'illness,' can it be blamed for enlisting in its support, a misinformed caricature of the Church's inadequate and unbalanced view of prophecy? Sadly, the second psychiatrist was of non-indigenous, perhaps Muslim provenance, and as such, his 'Western, medical' world view might, perhaps, have been further nuanced, leading to his medical recommendation that Chris be detained once again, under Section 3 of the Mental Health Act.

So called aberrant behavior by Chris may first have been picked up by her social workers, presumably following her confidences during counselling sessions, and especially those concerning her/our relations with our new church. Fifteen months into our membership of the church, an issue had arisen which was subsequently to lead to the effective breakup of the fellowship. In its essence, the problem concerned the use of the church building (in return for a fee), by a television production company whose efforts created a religious drama series, which was eventually screened on national TV. The drama series was less than edifying for the Christian faith, and could in no sense be said to have brought glory to God. We were forthright in speaking out against the venture, claiming authoritative revelation from the LORD in our support, and significantly, building upon a much earlier prophecy from within the congregation, which had predicted a church split. Sadly, the whole thing was so unnecessary, since the church was a fairly wealthy fellowship having no need of the fee offered, rather it was driven by certain egos who carried the decision in the church meetings. Our subsequent vindication came after we had left the church, and it gave us no joy to see an erstwhile, thriving church reduced to a leaderless group, one third its previous size. At the time, however, Chris's confidences to her social workers concerning this dissension, were no doubt presenting to the secular mind as psychosis, meriting immediate referral to the psychiatrists.

Communication with God—Cowardice

On the day after the visit from the second psychiatrist, we found ourselves descended upon by what can only be described as the medical and social services equivalent of a 'SWAT' team. Two consultant psychiatrists having now suggested that Chris was suffering from a 'religious' psychosis, that this was supplementary to her depression, and that there was an ongoing need for compulsory detention in hospital, had clearly invoked a 'team handed' domiciliary visit. We found assembled before us that afternoon, the GP, Chris's social worker and an authorized social worker (ASW), that is, one with the power to authorize compulsory committal under Mental Health Act Section. The encounter turned into a traumatic confrontation, during which these professionals attempted to persuade me to agree to have Chris detained under Section. The normal 'line up' for such a compulsory detention usually comprises the GP or psychiatrist, an ASW and the nearest relative of the subject. This meant that it was incumbent upon the assembled professionals to convince both the subject, and the near relative, of the pressing need for hospitalisation. It is necessary in such circumstances to isolate the subject within his/her societal matrix from as many (at least three) perspectives as possible, and perhaps additionally, also convince him/her of the efficacy of the proposed course of action.

In this regard, they singularly failed to convince me of the need to detain Chris, but I did display a measure of cowardice in the face of their combined, conventional, secular 'wisdom.' Indeed, in my desire to appear 'reasonable' and 'conciliatory,' I allowed myself to be overpowered by their worldly arguments, and so deny my *own* knowledge of the spiritual realities I shared with Chris. The GP's medical record written up the next day, notes that Chris *admitted* to having 'religious delusions,' although the word 'delusion' had never been used in any of the psychiatrist's reports. Perhaps I too would have been branded delusional, had I more fully supported Chris, and this could have opened the way for the professionals to use Section 29 of the Mental Health Act to bypass me as nearest relative. In branding Chris's expressed views on her relationship with the LORD as delusional, the doctor had applied her own interpretation and loaded value judgement to the situation. Such a position, although technically supported by Chris's apparent isolation from 'mainstream' views, goes well beyond a defensible professional stance, and more properly indicates a clash of worldviews. The encounter was effectively between a modern world view, exemplified by a secularly trained, professional laboring under her own personal misunderstandings, and a much older concept of the world—one in which God was *personally* interactive. An inability to acknowledge or comprehend the possibility of external spiritual communication to a human being reflects the legacy bequeathed by the mechanistic science of the eighteenth and nineteenth centuries. Fortunately, as the 'modern' gives way to the 'post modern,' this outdated concept of the cosmos is being superseded by a newer, more spiritually orientated view, not unlike that which preceded the modern age.

Whatever else Chris did or did not 'admit' to that afternoon, it could not be denied that she had declared that she continued to harbor suicidal inclinations, and on that basis the assembled professionals then pressed her to agree to a voluntary admission. This compromise solution defused the situation, and with discretion being the better part of valor, Chris allowed herself to be admitted to the hospital late that afternoon. Just one week later, however, Chris discharged herself in like manner, and settled down to begin a long period of outpatient care under the supervision of a consultant psychiatrist. Apparently, the difficulties of retaining Chris in hospital now became resignedly accepted, and the main thrust of her 'treatment' from this point forward was by psychopharmacological means, on an outpatient basis. In other words, a drug regime was instigated to change what were now understood—by secular physicians and psychiatrists—to be *abnormal psychotic beliefs of a religious nature*. Nevertheless, effectively a truce had been agreed in the war between worldviews, provided Chris kept taking the pills!

Communication with God—Disbelief

The anorexia continued to recede throughout the autumn, and by the early spring of 1994 Chris's weight had recovered to a more normal range of eight to nine stone, although this was undoubtedly assisted by the metabolic side effects of the drug regime. It was a bad winter though, especially in terms of our relationship with the LORD, and Chris began to reject the 'body language' giftings, that were such an integral part of her revelations. The denial coincided with, or more accurately followed the final break with the church, which itself was precipitated by a domiciliary visit of a different kind. This meeting with the pastor was also confrontational, and Chris uncompromisingly presented the prophetic picture, as it had been built up from all the various inputs, including our own, over the past twelve months. He was told in no uncertain terms, that he had taken a 'wrong turn,' but that it was still not too late to repent and, moreover, lead the church in repentance for its inglorious participation in the controversial television programme. The outcome of that meeting was both predictable and inevitable, and we soon found that pastoral authority had been applied, preventing our friends in the prayer group from associating with us—at least in any Christian capacity as a group. Now there is a self-validating anecdote often found circulating in churches, that likens the church to a fire made up of individual embers or coals, and warns that coals which fall out of the fire invariably go out. Essentially, such a view depends on an identity between that which men consider to be the church, and that which God considers to be the church. The two may not always be the same, and the idea that the *local* church is identical with the (whole) body of Christ can be a potentially manipulative and dangerous position to adopt. In our own case, the appropriation of such a notion was completely foreign to the way in which we had come to faith, and also to our ongoing relationship with the LORD. Thus, our faith remained intact, indeed became strengthened, although we began to question those 'body language' aspects, which had been considered so 'beyond the pale.' Chris, especially began to doubt her 'creep,' and angrily asked the LORD to take the gift away again, whilst I allowed the elaborate system of 'buzzes' and 'lifts' that had been devised to fall into disuse.

The problem, however, had nothing to do with these particular giftings, but had rather more to do with our naïve utterance of (all of) the revelations we received. It was the (my) old problem revisited, that is, a tactless inability to function as political animals in a small organisation. But then this wasn't just any body politic—it was a part of the body of Christ, and irrespective of the consequences, we had blurted out all that we had received from the LORD in perfect faithfulness. The result was ostracism and it hurt. After a little less than two years, the local church, and especially our friends in the prayer group, had become almost our entire life. In our pain we had rejected the giftings, and in so doing we were effectively rejecting the Holy Spirit, since to reject the manifestations of the Spirit is to reject the Spirit himself, although we were not conscious of this identity at the time. In our desire to be rid of the perceived root of our pain we risked rejecting life itself, yet we never felt in the least bit distanced from our LORD during this time, and we continued to feel completely at one with Him. To be fully understood by God in this way is one of the greatest consolations of the Christian faith, and as our pain eased with the passage of time, we were able to relent of our earlier rashness.

Beginning with the break with our church, it is clear that 1994 was a momentous year in which just about everything in our lives changed. To begin with our teetering business finally crashed to the ground, doing so in two stages. Firstly, the general insurance side of the business was 'sold' off to another broker, which effectively meant that the renewals were transferred *en bloc*, whilst we continued to receive 'renewal' income for a limited period. Later on, the financial services side was 'sold' to a another financial services company on a similar basis, but this company failed to make good on its promises and subsequently also went out of business. We received in total perhaps £84.00 from them, but because they would not indemnify the life assurance companies against advance commissions received by us in the past, much of our business was not transferred to them and we continued to receive renewal income. Thus, for a limited period we had a trickle of income available to offset some of the demands of dozens of creditors, but not nearly enough to prevent the whole 'house of cards' from collapsing. Eventually, the mortgage company could not be put off any longer and called in the debt, sealing the property up only a matter of days after we had left. The LORD was especially active at this time, giving us a very 'soft landing' in a small, rented, terraced cottage, that was situated in the quietest location imaginable—an important consideration given Chris's continuing depression.

The physical evidence of the whole of my forty eight years on this planet had been methodically dismantled, and I was learning that there is no security outside the LORD. It is at such times, that a (wo)man needs his God, and after six years of unremitting illness followed by a breakup with our church friends, we simply had no one else. All our secular friends and family had cooled in their interest towards us, and their visits to our home diminished to vanishing point. Social contact now consisted almost entirely of the 'round' of GPs, psychiatrists, CPNs and social workers, whilst work had been replaced by the constant need to complete benefit application forms of one sort or another. During the last months at our old home, I still felt I had some need of a new church relationship—perhaps a perceived need for ongoing Christian teaching. In any event, I began to attend a local Anglican church, firstly alone, but later to be joined by Chris, and I remember yet another domiciliary visit, this time by our new vicar. We sat the vicar down—cup of tea in hand—and his face was a picture as I told him how "I get these feelings in my hands you know . . ."

8

Kept Up All Night!

AT THE END OF 1994 our erstwhile world had completely collapsed, for in addition to losing our home to repossession we had neither business nor job between us, and we owed perhaps £125,000 to creditors of one sort or another. Moreover, it wasn't possible for me to seek employment given Chris's suicidal depression, and so I settled down to accepting my new 'official' role as her Full Time Carer. The British government acknowledges the importance of full time carers by paying them a welfare benefit known as "(Invalid) Care Allowance," in return for a minimum 35 hours care work per week. Indeed, each full time carer probably saves the state between £1500 and £2000 per week, by assuming the role of up to a dozen paid professionals, and by caring for their charge in the community—thereby avoiding the accommodation and board costs of state owned facilities. In return for this service, the State remunerates carers via the Care Allowance, at the rate of about £1.34 per hour, equivalent to about a quarter of the Statutory Minimum Wage. This benefit ceases, as do most other benefits when the carer's charge is hospitalized for six weeks or more, on the rationale that the state has (re)assumed all the responsibility and costs of the care of the subject. Cessation of benefits in this manner became an issue for us, when towards the end of the year, Chris was asked by her psychiatrist to agree to a voluntary admission to hospital, in order to undergo drug evaluation trials.

The reason for this, put at its simplest, was that the psychiatrist needed a safe and controlled environment, in which to firstly discontinue all existing drug therapy, before instituting and evaluating a new drug regime. Unfortunately, such a programme requires large amounts of time, since the existing drug, which is bound to the body's receptor sites, must be disengaged from, or 'washed out' of the subject's system. This must then be followed by a further lengthy period, in which the new drug regime is allowed to 'bond' to the same or other receptor sites, before its efficacy can then be evaluated. The consultant psychiatrist was made aware of the 'six week' benefit rule, and agreed to Chris spending weekends at home in order to extend his evaluation period to eight weeks, whilst simultaneously protecting our (only) household income. A good working relationship was built up with the consultant during this period, and it later became apparent that it was at about this time, that he began a shift in his thinking concerning Chris. Thoughts of 'religious psychosis' were left behind, and his efforts turned towards investigating the relationship between chronic fatigue syndrome and long term resistive depression. Of course, it may have been simply good psychology on his part, designed to reassure Chris that she was being listened to, but nevertheless, he was as good as his word and subsequently arranged a (day patient) referral to a CFS unit at a nearby university hospital. The net result of the in-patient stay was that a stable, new drug regime was put in place, and Chris came home for Christmas, with the prospect of a diagnosis of CFS, that is, a final vindication—not least to the GP—of all she had been through during the past six years.

Modest Plans

Although we were wary of forming meaningful relationships following the trauma of the church breakup, we found that we were easily assimilated into the friendly new Anglican church fellowship. Friendships were quickly formed, despite there being a high turnover (due to job mobility) in the largely professional congregation, and I felt more hopeful for the future than I had done for some years past. Despite occasional crises of extremely low mood, Chris remained relatively stable, although she still mourned the passing of what she felt had been a useful and active life. I too felt excluded from society in a strange way, and although this feeling persisted for the better part of two years, I felt sufficiently optimistic to begin to think about the future. Clearly, the practicalities of caring for Chris would remain paramount for some years yet, but I wondered whether there was some activity I could engage in, which would dovetail unobtrusively with her care. It was during a church performance by a well known, Christian 'pop' group, that I had one of those blinding flashes of inspiration, which bring crystal clarity to any situation. As I was enjoying the very physical and well choreographed songs, what struck me was the very great similarity between the group's forceful proclamation of the Gospel message, and my erstwhile occupation as a salesman. Some years previously I had been struck by a similar connection *vis-à-vis* the teaching career I had not followed, and the insurance sales career I had followed. The single factor which connected all three together was the ability to communicate, or more particularly, *to present* a body of information in an easy and readily absorbed manner. It came as a revelation to me that this Christian band were doing a presentation—something with which I was very familiar, after eleven years spent in business for myself. The next step in the revelation process was putting 'two and two together,' in my own personal circumstances. In a nutshell, I was skilled at making presentations—albeit often in a one to one situation—and I was a trained teacher. All this thinking took place in seconds, or more accurately, in the time it took the group's lead singer to spring a handstand off the communion rail!

It didn't take too much longer to draw further conclusions, and it seemed obvious that I should embark upon a theology degree course, in order to be able—upon Chris's full recovery—to teach Religious Education in secondary schools. At the time, it seemed that this would be the way in which I would honor my Christian committal vow, since I would then be able to serve the LORD as a trained teacher in two shortage subjects. What could be a more ideal, Christian service, than to contribute towards a reconciliation of the perceived antagonism between science and theology? But there were doubts, doubts about my vocation for teaching obnoxious, disinterested 'third formers,' especially as an older man, well past the first flush of youthful energy. Fully three or four years away from graduation, I was able to thrust these doubts to the back of my mind, as I began to concentrate on getting acceptance onto an appropriate course.

Filled with enthusiasm, I quickly obtained an interview for undergraduate admission at a nearby university, and duly met with the course tutor in his office. The venue for my studies needed to be very local, that is, within easy commuting distance of home, in order to combine study with my caring responsibilities. Consequently, I was utterly devastated when I was told in no uncertain manner, that both my age and my science background militated against my successful completion of the course. It seemed I was 'over the hill' at forty nine years of age, and it was felt that I would be unfamiliar with theological essays, indeed essays of any kind, and quite unable to complete them to the standard expected by the university. This seemed to put an end to my modest ambitions, until an advertizement in an evangelical magazine was brought to my attention, by our vicar. Apparently, he had recently attended an open day at a nearby Christian college, which intended to widen its intake of students to include all 'evangelicals,' and it was their advertizement that he pointed out to me. I duly applied to the college, obtaining an interview with both the dean and the principal, and was subsequently accepted onto their four year long, undergraduate course, subject only to my raising the better part of £12,000 in tuition fees!

The Alpha Course

The phenomenal success of the a Course—the 'brainchild' of Holy Trinity Brompton—is now well known, especially following its screening on national TV as introduced by David Frost. In the nineteen nineties, however, the a Course was only just beginning to become a trans-denominational teaching resource, which could be used as a complete course in the basics of Christianity. The written guidelines for the ten week course could be followed, by using either the church's own resources, or by making use of the video material supplied with the 'a Course kit.' Frequently, the videos— which depicted a series of presentations by Nicky Gumbel—would be used, not least because the only pieces of equipment required were a domestic video machine and a television set. Sometimes, however, where a church could field competent presenters, and in addition, possessed visual teaching aids such as whiteboards, flip charts, reprographics, and OHP's, it would attempt a more comprehensive course. It was to such an a Course that we were attracted that summer. Despite having been a Christian for more than three years, I felt that I needed the benefit of a structured presentation of the basic tenets of the faith, since even as a church 'home group' member, I felt I had only acquired an *ad hoc* knowledge from bible studies. Moreover, it seemed that I was not alone in this view, since the local a Courses seemed in the main to attract Christians of many years standing, together with some others from a church background. Indeed, those with little or no connection with the faith seemed very much in the minority.

So it came about that shortly after 8 pm on a Tuesday evening in June, Christine and I attended one particular a Course meeting, having as its subject, the Holy Spirit. The meeting began, appropriately enough, with two choruses welcoming the Holy Spirit, and it was at this point, that I felt a 'tingling' sensation in my hands that I can only further describe as a 'flux' or 'field' which builds in intensity. It is in fact an extremely pleasurable feeling, and always tells me that the Spirit is present, irrespective of where I am at the time. The pastor began his talk at perhaps 8.20 or 8.25 pm, and

I mentally took issue with him on two points. Firstly, he vehemently described graduates of university theology departments and bible colleges, as often being devoid of the Holy Spirit. This troubled me, since I had just been offered such a place at bible college, and naturally, I fervently hoped that the fate he described could be avoided. Secondly, in his description of prayer in tongues, he had indicated that such prayer, 'bypassed the brain,' and whilst fully agreeing with him, I still found myself making the mental note: "Yes, but don't leave your mind in neutral"! The talk was followed by a coffee break, and after coffee the meeting split off into separate groups, each numbering about six in all. A discussion on the Holy Spirit ensued, revealing that some of the group members were currently subject to undisclosed secular pressures. During a period of open prayer, I prayed (silently) for the Holy Spirit to 'come in power' on the group, and especially those in distress. I was amazed to feel the 'tingling sensation'—which had returned at the commencement of this prayer time—intensify to engulf my whole body, so much so, that at one point I felt in danger of falling off my chair! I remember noting, that while I was praying silently, the group leader was praying audibly for the Holy Spirit to touch each one of us. As the prayer time closed, I recall feeling both drained and yet sated—at one and the same time, and proceeded to leave the meeting with Chris, but without mentioning my experience. On the way home I poured out, in great elation, my experience to Chris, and I feel sure that had a policeman followed our car, I would have been stopped and breathalyzed—such was my elation and associated erratic driving! It was about a quarter past ten when we arrived home, and my 'high spirits' persisted—much to my son's embarrassment, and his friend's puzzlement!

The Night

We retired to bed about an hour later, but did not go to sleep immediately, as it had become Chris's normal practice to meditate for perhaps 30 minutes at this time. Then, towards the end of this period, she abruptly announced, "we must read 1 Samuel 3 in the morning." Understandably perhaps, I asked why and was told—"it just popped into my head." I was filled with such curiosity that I decided not to wait until morning, and instead got up to retrieve the nearest bible. 1 Samuel 3 depicts Samuel "in the LORD's service" under Eli the priest, that is, undergoing instruction, and emerging by the chapter's end as "a trustworthy prophet of the LORD" known throughout Israel. The import of the text was that my first mental query—raised during the pastor's address—had been answered by the LORD. In particular, yes—it was possible to survive even a bad theology instruction/training course and still be in touch with the Holy Spirit! The LORD was making it clear that even poor quality training, as received by Samuel under the decadent Eli (1 Sam. 2), cannot shut out the Holy Spirit from those who are spiritually open. Feeling suitably amazed, I attempted to go to sleep, only to be awakened 15 minutes later by Chris again asking for the bible. This time it was 1 Corinthians 10:14–15 that had just 'popped into her head,' and the particular sentences that stood out were: "I speak to you as men of sense. Form your own judgement on what I say." Clearly, this was a direct answer to my second reservation during the pastor's address, which if understood in our (1995) context, might be paraphrased as "you are reasonable men, measure my word against your science and philosophy,"—without neglecting the use of all the gifts of the Spirit. Interestingly, the first verse (1 Cor. 10:14) speaks simultaneously to a commonly observed failing of the charismatic community, who, in following their Pentecostal forebears, have tended to venerate or idolize the gift of speaking in tongues. In this I suspect the LORD was reassuring *me* personally, since at that time I had never uttered a single word in a tongue, and I felt it was quite ridiculous to attempt to practice this gift, as many had suggested I do. Practicing tongues, it seemed to me was exactly that, nothing more than *cryptomnesia*—the utterance of a jumbled up mixture of half remembered foreign languages. Having said this, it (much) later became a part of my (very brief!) private prayer times to practice utterance of tongues, in just this way so that when the real need of such prayer arose, there would be no inhibitions. I discovered that there was always a difference between the practiced cryptomnesia of those private prayer sessions, and true tongues, which have a quality, character, and coherence of a quite different order. Indeed, I can count the latter occasions on the fingers of both hands.

By now of course, it was well after two in the morning and I had become completely bemused by the immanence of this (Spirit of) God, who had stood beside me throughout the evening, had listened to me and had then replied in detail through Chris to all my queries. It was quite clear that Chris had known nothing of my mental queries during the pastor's address, until after the scripture passages had been given to her and read out, for it was only then that I told her of them. Moreover, immediately following the giving of the two bible texts, and before finally going to sleep, I had told Chris that I expected her to have a third verse given to her. This, because Samuel had been awakened three times by the LORD. But it wasn't until the late afternoon of the following day that Chris confirmed in incidental conversation, that this third verse had in fact been given. Chris had simply been too tired to get up again and tell me about the third verse—Romans

2:27, which when paraphrased and personalized to our context can read: "The churchman who follows traditional precepts (i.e. established orthodoxy) will denounce you, who, by learning (knowledge) and consecration to God, are a breaker of long established conventions within the church." It was gradually becoming clear that as well as answering my queries from the a Course evening, the unfolding sequence of verses could be seen as having a personal 'predictive' quality about them. In other words the LORD was forth telling his intentions with regard to our lives, which had of course been surrendered to him. In short, those intentions were that I would study theology and marry this body of knowledge seamlessly with the science I already had, doing all whilst still remaining spiritually open and available. Moreover, this would bring me into conflict with other churchmen, over certain long established points of dogma held by the Western Catholic Church. I was much later to ruefully recall this forth telling when brought to task by a brother Christian, following a bible study I gave touching on the nature of sin.

The Lord's Will Revealed

The events of that June night seemed to confirm that the LORD's will for me (us), over the next four years was to study theology, but why had He only 'shown his hand' at this late stage—long after I had been accepted onto the theology course? All along I had felt it was right to make the application, but in truth, I was doing it more because of personal gratification or perhaps the (childlike) thrill of discovering truth, than any altruistic reasons of service. It seems, however, that the LORD needed me to be walking in the right direction, before disclosing that this was the direction He intended *Us* to walk together! Once that disclosure had commenced—with those first three verses, an ongoing and ever deepening revelatory process was put in train, which eventually became even more dialogical in character. The way in which this first disclosure was made speaks volumes about 'the LORD's will,' which is less about determinism, and more about a cooperative walk with God involving enjoyment, gratification, and edification. I was later to discover that the Greek word for 'will,' *thelema*, can also be translated as 'wish'—a considerably weaker term, which implies that God's good desires are, at least to some extent, contingent upon the level of cooperation He receives. Success, it seems, would be assured if God's good desires can become synonymous with his servant's good desires, and therefore, I needed to appropriate this particular 'good desire' for myself, before He disclosed how it was his idea all along!

I was so excited by these revelatory verses, that I wrote them all down in detail the next day, giving a copy to our minister, who wasn't exactly overwhelmed! As a new(ish) Christian I felt that they might have been important to our relationship with our church, and so I had hoped that older, wiser heads would be able to see the import of these words more clearly than I. In the event, I felt rather childish when the transcript was dismissed with a comment along the lines of; "people get verses like these all the time, its not exceptional," before it was passed on to the minister. But this wasn't simply a case of new Christians thinking that every verse they read was prophetic for them personally. Despite the chagrined response, Chris wasn't searching the bible for 'inspiration,' rather these verses were coming uninvited by named chapter and verse number. The significance of the verses was that firstly they were direct answers to *mental queries*, whilst secondly forming a sequence in *our personal context*—as quite distinct from the scriptural one—which forth told a story, and thirdly affirmed an already initiated course of action. Sadly, the minister never got back to me, and so almost imperceptibly, a process began in which all my thinking about Christianity started to take place outside my church, reinforcing the commonly held perception that church and academy are utterly separate. Later on, I was to come across gifted teachers in various institutions, whose heartfelt desire was to end this 'never the twain shall meet' syndrome in our churches. Included in the transcript given in to church was a final (fourth) verse, which Chris had received during a meditation the following day. The final verse was 1 Corinthians 4:12, which might be paraphrased: "We are to work hard with all the means at our disposal. When (verbally) abused, we should bless, when harassed, we should bear up and maintain our self respect." In the context of the impending theology course, this seemed to be good advice for the future. With regard to that course, however, there remained a big question mark: How was it to be financed?

The first port of call when raising money for study—at least before the phasing out of student grants in Britain—was obviously the Local Education Authority, and I had already submitted an application to them. Having already been in receipt of a mandatory grant, albeit fully 25 years earlier, I had applied for a discretionary grant but had been turned down for this also. The next thing to do was to invoke the appeals procedure, which I did, even enlisting the support of my local councillors and MP, but this too was to be of no avail. All through these days in late June, the verses initiated on the a Course night continued to flow profusely, providing guidance of every kind, and as we waited for the appeal result I briefly considered applying for a student loan. The student loan system which had been set up at that time, was running parallel with the soon to be dropped student grant system, and as we discussed this possibility Chris received yet another verse, Deuteronomy 24:6. Paraphrased into our context, this verse might read: "Do not pledge what will ultimately become your living (degree course) or indeed any part of it, because to do so would be to pledge life itself." I took the point and abandoned the idea of applying for a loan. At the end of June the news finally came that the appeal had been denied, and needless to say, this precipitated me into deep despondency. Specific, contextually relevant verses continued to come, however, always in direct response to our thoughts and prayers, and they encouraged me to investigate the possibilities of obtaining a grant from the various charitable trusts listed in the library. I was not optimistic, but eventually submitted two or three applications, mostly to Christian charitable trusts, and throughout, the verses flowed giving encouragement. After about two months had passed with no word concerning these applications, it was quite natural to doubt the whole thing, and towards the end of August—only two weeks from the start of the new term—I voiced my doubts about the verses to Chris. The response was immediate, and we felt suitably rebuked as Chris received 2 Timothy 3:16. Two weeks later I enrolled on the course with only a few hundred pounds towards the cost of the tuition fees, and it wasn't until the end of that week, that I received the news that I had been awarded £3,000 for each of the four years of the course!

9

Good Science—Bad Theology

THE FIRST WEEK AT bible college was something of a revelation in more ways than one. To begin with, the age range of the students was truly staggering, and I found myself in the middle of that range, which extended from fresh-faced eighteen year olds to a retired librarian aged seventy plus. Indeed, with the bulk of the class over thirty years of age, the youngsters were in the minority. The first week was something of an induction week in which we were able to worship together, to brush up on study skills, and be advised of the career prospects for a (young?) theology graduate. One lecturer informed us that a career in air traffic control was to be included amongst those opportunities, bringing to mind endless puns on Paul's words in 1 Thessalonians 4:17!

Moreover, it soon became apparent that the college was striving towards financial viability in its own right, and now had its highest ever number of full time students enrolled. This was important because the original function of the college had been to train pastors for ordination into the denomination's own pastorate. The shrinking numerical base of the denomination—at least in the UK—had meant that the maintenance of a teaching college establishment was now proving onerous, causing the college to begin to widen its (fee paying) intake. Indeed, to the uninitiated observer, this obscure college might have appeared to be the training base of some fundamentalist cult, or at the very least, the Wesleyan equivalent of the Jesuits! Eventually, however, I came to realize that within this small college, there was access to arguably the best bible teaching in the UK, albeit taught by a staff augmented by Canadians and Americans, and led by an Irishman. Over time, it also became apparent that many of the staff engendered an analytical and empirical approach to both their teaching, and their personal research, which proved to be quite refreshing.

For some students this approach seemed to be controversial, perhaps even verging on the heretical, and induced many a passionate class discussion from amongst the half dozen denominational perspectives represented there. Many would argue that one of the primary objectives of teaching any subject is the creation of a stimulating debate within the class, and the achievement of this objective may be deemed to be one measure of a successful teaching strategy. The situation was further complicated (or enriched?) by the composition of the class, which could include second, third, and fourth year students, as well as freshers, depending on the particular module being studied. Very few of the students (or indeed the staff) would, however, have considered themselves to be 'charismatics,' as the term is conventionally understood. Thoroughgoing debate on this aspect of the contemporary Christian scene was conspicuous by its absence.

Back to School

The first year at college was the typical 'foundation' year familiar to all freshers, and in hindsight it could be seen to have been superfluous for me, especially given the college's policy to give accreditation to other students for their past work. Perhaps it was that same prejudice against a scientific background—as opposed to an arts background—which had prevented the college from offering me a one year remission from the course's full length of four years. Looking back it seemed that little account had been taken of the sociology, psychology and the like, which had formed a part of my Post Graduate Teaching Certificate, and which now comprised a significant part of this first foundation year. Having said this, however, I thoroughly enjoyed that first year, chiefly because I had never studied in that way before. All my previous studies had been vocationally oriented courses, driven by the eventual need to earn a living, with the scientific curriculum carefully selected for appropriateness to the technological environment of the workplace. It now became possible to study modern/post modern society from outside, without that society or its worldview significantly intruding into the study process. I am not here advocating an 'ivory towers' approach to university education, but while fully approving of pragmatic, 'feet on the ground' academies, I nevertheless feel a certain distance is necessary, indeed essential, to good tertiary education. In short, my foundation year provided me with considerably more objectivity about the society in which we live, than had hitherto been the case. Educational philosophy, however, was not uppermost in my mind, when, at the end of that first year, I came to sit the exams and found to my great disdain, that I was obliged to sit (again!) what was effectively an English Language "O" level!

Amongst the modules that comprised the curriculum during the first term was one named "Spiritual Formation," which as its name suggests, endeavored to come to grips with Christian spirituality. I still have difficulty with this term, spirituality, since it describes a subtle, and quite indefinable blend of personality, theology, and discipline, which although incapable of formulation, remains instantly identifiable in those that possess it. As one of a number of disciplines comprising their personal spiritual formation, all the students were encouraged to keep a journal, and it was suggested that this could be an electronic journal recorded onto floppy disc, in order to stimulate budding diarists. I felt that I could manage this near effortless means of keeping a diary, and began to commit my thoughts to magnetic record each evening. I decided from the outset, that I would record only those incidents worthy of note, if only to avoid a nightly impasse at the keyboard, spent struggling to recall anything of significance from the day's events. At first, this meant that only about half a dozen, dated entries were made in the journal each month, and these most frequently recalled interactions with other Christians, through whom God seemed to be speaking. One such incident actually took place towards the end of a college night class, when the lecturer asked if any of us had ever experienced the glory of God. Some students immediately said yes, but I was only able to think that I had experienced the presence of God—not the glory. The class closed and as I turned to leave, a fellow student, with whom previously I had only passed pleasantries, said to me: "You know the glory of God simply means the presence of God"! It seemed that I had just had my conception of the word 'glory' corrected by God, and later research revealed that the Hebrew root of the word was "weight," or "heaviness," and this is completely consistent with my personal experience of the presence of God. Later studies were to demonstrate that 'glory' was not the only word to have suffered corruption since ancient times.

I had started the journal in the first month of the first term at college, but by March the following year, the character of the entries had begun to change, as more and more reference was made to the verses Chris was now receiving on a regular basis. Whereas in the earliest months, the journal entries had typically numbered four or five, they now began to increase exponentially, often recording tripartite conversations involving the LORD's interjections. One example that particularly exemplifies this was a family discussion concerning our future, and prompted by my recent return to college. Those half buried doubts about teaching religious education were unearthed, when my sister asked a penetrating question about my career intentions following the completion of the course. I was put on the spot, but answered that there were two options: Firstly, I could go into teaching as originally planned, or alternatively, I could go into the Church. As I reeled from the import of having voiced that second option, Chris interjected with a third alternative: I could become a writer. During her meditation that night Chris received the single verse, 2 Samuel 24:12, which reads: "Go and say to David: Thus says the LORD: Three things I offer you; choose one of them, and I will do it to you." Being an indecisive sort of person, I handed this particular decision back to the LORD in prayer, but this kind of 'eavesdropping' by the LORD became increasingly commonplace from this time onwards.

The *modus operandi* of this eavesdropping function can differ, and one occasion in particular stands out when the LORD's interjection into our discussion was given in a 'tongue.' I was about half way through my college course at the time, and Chris and I were holidaying together in mainland Greece—the southern Peloponnese in fact. It was hot, even the Greek news service said it was hot, and to avoid the midday heat we would often go on sailing trips to the nearby islands. On this particular trip, having spent two hours or so in the air-conditioned lounge of the motor vessel, we disembarked into the early afternoon heat of the island of Hydra. After walking ten paces we were sapped of all our energy, and staggered to a shady back street café for a light, late lunch. With lunch over and the temperature nudging 44° C, we were desperate to find some activity offering brief respite from the heat, until it was time to leave the island. Although we could have spent this interval under the canopies of the harbor shops, we decided to visit the island's sixteenth century Greek Orthodox church. Immediately upon entering the building we were enveloped in the coolness we were seeking, and began to examine our surroundings uninterrupted by other tourists. The church was effectively a large, single room in which the congregation stood (for there were no chairs present) around two high pulpits, which were reached by spiral staircases winding round two supporting pillars. Alcoves indented all four walls at regular intervals, and in each were hung the heavily soiled portraits of past saints. The fact that the empty church seemed so featureless, might have been what prompted me to make an observation to Chris along the lines of: "The Spirit of God seems to be absent here, perhaps the worship is very formal, rigid, and lifeless." Seated on the bottom rung of one of the spiral staircases Chris replied with the words: "*Christos est Dios.*"

I wrote those words down, together with the further words, "*Logos ultra Domini,*" that Chris uttered when again at her ease in the ship's lounge later on. The two phrases seemed at first sight to be a crazy mixture of Greek, Latin, and modern Spanish, none of which had ever been within the ambit of Chris's Secondary Modern school curriculum! Indeed, fresh as I was from my New Testament Greek module, I too struggled with these words since I had little Spanish and no Latin, and it took fully two years before the words came to make any kind of sense. In the event, the word *Dios* which I had taken to be the Spanish word for God, turned out to be a synonym for Zeus mentioned in Acts 14:13 of the Greek New Testament, and having the meaning '*the god of all the Greeks*'. Thus, in response to my scepticism concerning the faith of the congregation on Hydra the LORD had effectively replied: "*Christos est Dios—I, the Messiah or Christ, am the God of all the Greeks.*" The second phrase also seems to be a curious mixture of Greek and Latin, which to some extent continues to puzzle me, but it occurred to me that both languages might have been familiar to the first century (multilingual, seafaring?) inhabitants of this Greek island. Moreover, the full meaning of *Logos* is incapable of a comprehensive translation into either Latin or English, since in addition to '*Word*,' it carries the meanings, '*Design*' and '*Logic*'. Putting the full message into paraphrase produces the awesome statement:

> *Christos est Dios. Logos ultra Domini.*
> *I, the Christ, am the God of all the Greeks. I am the ultimate*
> *Design lying beyond the (person(s) of the) Lords.*

This little episode in which Chris received a communication in a *recognisable* 'tongue/ tongues,' is somewhat different from the 'normal' perception of the gift of tongues, where words of an unknown language, *glossalalia*, are given. Indeed, this was the only time that either of us ever received a word in a known yet foreign language, that is, a personal experience of *xenolalia*.

The Enlightenment

Although diminished by my Christian experience, I had held a number of 'prejudices' from the days of my youth, and chief amongst these prejudices was a disdain for students of the 'Arts'. I had always felt that the 'arty farty' classes didn't have a clue about what was going on in the 'real' world, and needed compulsory instruction in the sciences, rather than it being the other way round, with mandatory General Studies content inserted into most science courses. It had always seemed to me that it was the scientists and technologists who had their feet firmly planted on the ground, who had broad interests in other subject areas, and who were thoroughly familiar with current affairs. In perfect hindsight, I can of course see the rationale, which induced the post-war education planners to introduce such content to science/technology courses. Clearly, there was fear that expansion of science education, driven as it was by the needs of industry, would produce a new, 'middle class', elite bereft of any civilising influences—cultural 'Philistines' in fact. So it was then, that I brought my residual grudges into that first year of my course, proceeding to take a superior—not to say aloof—perspective, especially during one particular module, which dealt with the development of Western thought.

The content of that module was concerned with the transition from medieval to modern philosophy, and how such thinking led ultimately to the development of the contemporary worldviews seen in our society today. Secular humanism, incorporating as it does scientific materialism, is one such worldview and one that dominates our modern Western world. The principle tenet of secular humanism is that human beings are free to exploit the universe for their own benefit, and that this 'right' was acquired by having achieved evolutionary supremacy. Such a reference to the theory of evolution was one of many oblique references, which were constantly being made throughout the module to 'science', and this always seemed to me to be 'tarring science with the same brush,' as the various aberrant philosophies. If one of the objectives of the module had been to enable students to evaluate alternative worldviews from within, then that would require assessment based on a *knowledge* of modern science, rather than the anachronistic, Newtonian, 'arts graduate's' *perception* of science. Perhaps I was being super sensitive, but the content of this and one or two other modules seemed to reinforce my abiding contention, that scientists were considerably more *au fait* with the arts than 'artists' (i.e. exponents of the humanities, social 'sciences' etc.) were with science.

Original Sin

In the second and subsequent years of the course, I began gradually to lose the scientific 'chip on my shoulder,' but not before I had brought my science into conflict with my lecturers' enlightened theology. I made the mistake (?) of submitting a Dogmatics paper, which offered a somewhat unique supporting view for the doctrine of the Immaculate Conception! The argument was based on the fact that in the human body the genetic material, DNA, (deoxyribonucleic acid), comes in two forms. Firstly, DNA is present in all of the genes which make up the chromosomes and which are specific to each individual man or woman. The full compliment of chromosomes possessed by a human being is forty six, contributed to equally by both parents during fertilisation, and they are located in the *nucleus* of the cell. The second source of DNA, resides in structures known as mitochondrial organelles, and these are situated in the body of the cell—the *cytoplasm*. During normal procreative fertilisation of the human egg (i.e. a single cell supplied exclusively by the woman), only the nuclear DNA is affected. Mitochondria, however, function as energy providers for cells, and as such, must be able to operate continuously, reproducing themselves independently of the nuclear fusion of fertilisation. Since they are located in the cytoplasm, external to the nucleus, their genetic material is not involved in the fertilisation process, and is passed from mother to daughter in an unbroken succession down the generations, *without ever involving male participation*. To the chagrin of the Paleontologists, some recent genetic research making use of this knowledge seems to indicate that human beings (*homo sapiens*) appeared approximately 200,000 years ago, somewhere in Africa. Indeed, as Pliny the Elder once exclaimed; *Ex Africa semper aliquit novi*—there is always something new out of Africa!

Thus, an intriguing possibility presents itself: Was Jesus 'conceived' by the Holy Spirit from Mary's mitochondrial genetic material, which had been received directly from the *pre-fall* Eve? I had, it seems, suggested a mechanism that supported a very Augustinian doctrine of original sin, one that was anathema to my lecturers, whose viewpoint I came to appreciate fully much later on. It seems, I had also obliquely hit upon a 'nerve,' that is, a tension which is somehow constantly present between nascent, biblical theology, and the derived, systematic theology of the Church—be that reformed or otherwise. The teaching staff, irrespective of their respective disciplines, all more or less held to a single ethos or 'philosophy,' which placed significantly more emphasis on biblical theology than on that which came later. Perhaps that is the way it should be in a bible college!

Apologetics and the New Science

'Apologetics' was another of the modules I took at college, which at first glance would seem to be the study of the science of 'saying sorry!' Unfortunately, this is yet another word that has significantly changed in meaning over the years of the Christian era, but its meaning in a theological context has remained constant. In a theological, or more especially a Christological context, the term 'Apologetics' has always meant the mounting of a cogent defence of a belief system, in this case Christianity. But what, it may be asked; must Christianity be defended from, in these early days of the third millennium? Certainly, much of the time allocation within the Apologetics module was given over to a study of the tension that exists between science and theology. Indeed, it seems as if thinking Christians have been in retreat before the onslaught of science for the better part of two hundred years. As already noted, many of those trained in the Arts and Humanities, together with the vast majority of the lay public, seem to share a very out of date perception of science—approximately 250 years out of date in fact.

Now this is precisely the problem—Christians are running away from a science which existed in the eighteenth century, and which no longer gives a full and satisfying explanation of the world around us! The sad fact is that apart from Darwin and his (unproven) theory of evolution, very little of the actual science of the past two hundred years has actually been absorbed into the corporate *psyche* of the public at large. Few can articulate the contributions of men like James Clerk Maxwell, or even more famous scientists such as Albert Einstein and Stephen Hawking. Mention of the second law of thermodynamics leaves most people cold, but interestingly, a full appreciation of its importance could revive one of the great Christian casualties of these past two centuries, reversing the demise of the biblical miracle. The second law of thermodynamics was postulated in the nineteenth century by James Clerk Maxwell, and provided a foundation for much later work including that of Einstein.

As its name suggests, the second law of thermodynamics is about heat, and heat is that quantity which arises as a result of the *motion* of the particles that make up the object. The faster or more energetic the motion of the particles or molecules, the higher the temperature of the object, and simply stated the second law describes the way in which that heat dissipates from a hotter to a colder body. The dissipation process involves the hotter, more energetic particles bumping into the cooler, slower ones, and becoming cooled themselves as a result. But, if it were possible to separate out the faster from the slower particles, then a *finite probability* exists of making a hot body hotter at the expense of a cold body—the complete reverse of all experience! This is, of course, impossible because the separating agency would have to have no mass or momentum, in order to prevent energetic interference with the particles concerned. Nevertheless, as Colin Russell points out, the existence of this theoretical 'chance' means that the second law is statistically based, as are all the many other scientific laws that utilize it in their derivation.

In short, all the things that we see around us in nature—governed as they are by the physical laws—only turn out to be the way they are on average, and the possibility of a different outcome always exists. As far as biblical miracles are concerned, this means that there is a finite chance or probability of a bizarrely different result ensuing from the natural laws, which govern every situation. Put simply, there is no need to invoke supernatural explanations for miracles, because there is a natural route to any desired outcome already built into nature, even though it would require a non-physical agent (God!) to bring it about.

Now it could be countered that all of this is hypothetical conjecture, and I certainly gave my imagination free reign during this time in college, but then why shouldn't thinking Christians use science (as a tool) as effectively as do their secular and atheist opponents? I have to admit that during these college years I neglected the study of the great systematic theologians—Barth, Brunner, Pannenburg *et al*, substituting instead readings of Davies, Tipler, Gribbin, and Penrose—the translators of the new science. Translation is of course vital, and involves rendering the language of mathematics into a readily assimilated format of contemporary English. These writers will often remark how graceful or elegant the mathematics is, and as a Chemist who had only a brief flirtation with A level calculus, I must take their word for this. Through their writings, I was able to haul my science into the twenty first century and place it at the service of my theology, rather than antithetically ranged against it.

Deutero Isaiah

Towards the end of the second year of the course I had completed some quite 'meaty' modules, and slowly, ever so slowly, I began to acquire an overview of the whole bible—the story of the people of God. In many respects I had a distinct advantage, in that I came to my theological studies unencumbered by a lifetime spent acquiring scripture 'sound bites,' for use in wholly inappropriate circumstances, after being wrenched from their contextual settings. In the main, however, I considered I had a vanishingly small store of chapter and verse, especially of the biblical links where scripture uses scripture. Nevertheless, my knowledge increased and I began to learn of the various positions held by scholars, concerning the origins of the books of the bible. The book of Isaiah is one example of a book where alternative views concerning its authorship are offered, mainly because the events portrayed in it take place at widely differing time periods. Two theories are offered entitled deutero and trito Isaiah, where proponents argue for two and three 'books' respectively.

The biggest consensus of scholars favor the former theory, and consider that Isaiah had two subjects, one in Jerusalem during the eighth century BC and one in Babylon during the sixth century BC.

Now this is one of those seemingly irrelevant pieces of information, which have little or no currency in the Church, after all, why should anyone give a fig about precisely when the events in the book of Isaiah actually transpired, or were written down! But, we were told at college (and parodying a famous election slogan), it's 'context! context! context!' that matters, even if only to theology students. Imagine then, my amazement when late in my second year at college, Chris told me that she had received a verse beginning 2 Isaiah, and that she had received others over the preceding weeks, but had disregarded them because, of course, *2 Isaiah does not exist*! I was only able to surmise that God knew that 2 Isaiah had existed—however transiently—before being amalgamated with the other (earlier?) work, into a single scroll. Needless to say, I spent the next day at college finding out precisely where in the sixty six chapters, Isaiah of Jerusalem finished and Isaiah of Babylon commenced, since it was vitally important that we were reading the correct verse. It turned out to be chapter thirty nine that closed the first 'book' of Isaiah, which left us ever afterwards with a little calculation to do! In the five years since that time, Chris has received some thousands of Isaiah verses and has never had 1 Isaiah exceed thirty nine, or 2 Isaiah exceed twenty seven.

10

Old Truths—New Contexts

THE STUDY OF SCIENCE, or indeed anything else, would be impossible if a full understanding of the terms used was lacking. Chemistry, which is often mystifying enough, would be opaque if students did not become familiar with such basic terms as crystallisation, precipitation, and the like. Above all the terms used must convey *exactly* the same concept to each practitioner. Sadly, this is not always the case in the Church, and one of the biggest problems borne by Christians is an imperfect understanding of the 'jargon words' the Church uses. To begin with, many words are never explained—they are simply preached, and even if the preacher assumes he is speaking to the congregational equivalent of a 'mixed ability class,' he rarely considers his text requires such a basic explanation. Home group bible studies, even though they stand 'knee deep' in study bibles similarly fail to contend with this issue, if only because the study bible footnotes likewise fail to explain the terms used. The result of this failure is that ordinary Christians are using words in contemporary situations, which have been plucked unchanged from their original settings. We believe we understand these words, and we believe everybody else does too, usually irrespective of how new the people are to Christianity! Thus, where a hundred Christians hold a hundred different concepts of the same term, the great danger is that of a complete communication breakdown, not least, between the 'old hand' and the newer convert.

One example that illustrates this perfectly can be found in Isaiah 53:11, in which the Suffering Servant, the Christ, is described as "my righteous servant (who) will justify many." A typical study bible entry would expand this phrase by simply restating that believers would become 'righteous,' because they have been 'justified' by accepting Christ, the one who takes away their sins. But this leaves the 'seeker' no further on, because the fundamental terms 'righteousness' and 'justification' are still not explained. A modern, lay understanding of the term 'righteousness' would run something along the lines of 'being in the right,' with 'justification' approximating to 'legal exoneration.' Such explanations would seem to fit in quite naturally with Jesus' trials before Pontius Pilate and Caiaphas. These meanings, however, whilst conveying an element of truth, fail to get to the heart of the matter, and part of the problem lies in the difficulty of finding a one-word equivalent for either term. 'Righteousness,' as understood by the gospel writers, had two slightly nuanced meanings in its Old Testament setting. Firstly, it referred to God's saving activity, whereby both nation and/or individual were saved or rescued. More frequently, however, it referred to God's maintained relationship with both Israel and various individuals within her. But these definitions are two sides of the same coin, since if men were in 'maintained relationship' with an Almighty, Eternal One, then they *must* necessarily be saved!

The Messiah or Christ of Isaiah 53:11 is God's Vice Regent on earth, holding fully delegated power to bring or restore relationship with God to all men through himself and thereby save them. Thus, the full meaning of 'justification' is to restore relationship, and it will therefore come as no surprise, that both 'righteousness' and 'justification' have the same root word (*dikai* . . .) in the New Testament Greek. Restoration of relationship (justification) in Old Testament times had always been the province of the (patriarchal) family, since in the days before the monarchy there was no state to assume, or indeed usurp that role. A typical extended family would number thirty to fifty persons, all of whom would work the land in some capacity or other, and every one of whom was essential to the economic viability of the whole. Conflict resolution by restoration of relationship, as quite distinct from legal exoneration, was fundamentally necessary to the survival of the unit, and the stark choice was cooperate or die! Interestingly, in the developed New Testament message, God offers much the same choice now through Jesus Christ.

The Hermeneutical Bridge

Hermeneutics is a discipline that should be familiar to anyone who has ever been asked to preach. It is about interpretation, that is, the identification and transfer of the essential, timeless principle from an ancient scriptural context to our own contemporary situation. The process of extracting and transferring this principle has been likened to constructing a link or bridge, across a cultural chasm. Although we have a Helper when we engage in this activity, we have a personal responsibility to the extent that we must try to study and understand the original cultural and political circumstances from which the text emerged. As already noted, if we are to understand what God is saying now, we need to know the 'jargon,' in order to cross the hermeneutical bridge! Words that have changed their meaning over time are said to have undergone a diachronic change, and this is easily illustrated with reference to two words long since absorbed into the English language. The word 'agnostic' (derived from the Greek) is normally used to describe a person who claims to have no knowledge of God, but the equivalent word 'ignoramus' (derived from the Latin) has an entirely different meaning in contemporary English! Although it may be objected that the original root words were never exact equivalents, it is nevertheless clear that marked divergence has occurred over the years since they had dual currency throughout the Mediterranean.

Knowing what a word meant in its own time and context—its synchronic meaning—is of fundamental importance to the task of crossing the hermeneutical divide, but becomes complicated by things like idiom, metaphor, apocalypticism, and hyperbole. Idiom and metaphor can be linked, and an expression peculiar to the original language and which need only be a single word, could have offered layers of meaning to its indigenous hearers that are lost to our generation. In this regard, I have always thought it odd that military terms appear to figure so little in the language of the New Testament. Indeed, the *Pax Romana* was held in place by a standing army (an entity unknown in history until this time!) of sixty five legions plus auxiliaries, and with upwards of half a million men under arms, things military must have been a daily reality for many people. This must have been especially so on the Greek and Macedonian mainland, which would have played a major role in the logistics of the Dacian (northern) frontier, as well as being the embarkation point for troops bound for Asia Minor. If, with F. F. Bruce we accept that Paul, the apostle to the Gentiles (Greeks), was familiar with military camps through his trade, then it becomes clear that the language of the New Testament will be imbued with such idiomatic, military metaphors. Perhaps there is sweet irony in Paul, the army chandler, walking the supply roads of the empire, and using military idioms to spread the gospel of peace!

The Apocalypse or Revelation of St. John is to most Christians 'the forbidden territory,' with its exotic picture language seemingly quite incapable of being understood. It is the supreme development of a genre of scripture known as apocalypticism, which has its roots in the writing prophets of the Old Testament. Ancient writers used the vivid language of apocalypticism to describe momentous events; events that very often involved massive social and political turmoil for the people involved. Such language, by its very use, signified the great importance of what was taking place. Apocalypticism in the writings of the prophets can often be found associated with hyperbole, which is a propensity towards great exaggeration found amongst Hebrew writers in particular. Hyperbole although emphasising the importance of the events described, frequently goes too far, and needs to be given a careful 'filtering' during any process of interpretation.

It was the acquisition of a rudimentary knowledge of such ancient literary devices, idioms, and genres, which slowly began to add greater layers of meaning to the verses Chris continued to receive. Almost imperceptibly the beginnings of questioning the LORD about the verse/word He had given were put in place, and the golden rule of never incorporating information from surrounding verses was strictly adhered to. This rule is essential because any widening of the given word draws the enquirer deep into the historical context, as distinct from the contemporary one that the LORD wishes to address. Besides, the amount of information packed into the average scripture verse is usually quite enormous, and is most definitely not in need of enlargement.

"Quiet Time"

In addition to building a knowledge base, the four years at college constituted a long period during which we began to pray together as a couple. Chris would bring a verse or word, which she had received, to my attention and this would result in both of us praying through it, often to be answered later the same day by a further verse. Thus, an attenuated or prolonged dialogue of sorts would ensue on most days, with the consequence that the so-called (and arguably unscriptural) "quiet time" became much reduced for both of us. Although we continued to pray privately, we were inexorably drawn into praying together as a couple—the fundamental unit of corporate prayer, and most decidedly against our natural inclinations. Moreover, we began to form prayer associations with some of our new 'Anglican' friends, as the trauma of separation from the old prayer group receded into the past. Gradually, when praying together as a couple and when praying in the new, wider group, we acquired greater 'skills' in this dialoguing process, until ultimately we were praying about every word we received.

Speaking about prayer, Jesus said, "When you pray, go into your room, close the door and pray to your Father, who is unseen. Then your Father, who sees what is done in secret, will reward you" (Matt. 6:6, NIV). At first, this would seem to validate our Western 'quiet times' which so suit our individualistic inclinations, but contextual considerations reveal that Jesus was condemning the hypocritical, public displays of prayer by vain men. Nevertheless, there does seem to be a place for private prayer in the life of the believer, but if this is so, why were we being led into an ever closer union in our prayer lives? The answer we arrived at, and which was a long time coming, seemed to revolve around the way in which the LORD regarded us. Put succinctly, He regarded us as being married, which seems to be a self-evident irrelevance until viewed from the perspective of Genesis 2:24, that is, 'one flesh.' It was clear He simply saw us as a single unit. This is not to say that our separate persons have ceased to exist, but rather that marriage involves a kind of spiritual union akin to that which exists within the Trinity—another example perhaps, of the *Imago Dei*. It was in fact a kind of 'both/and,' since we engaged in this nascent dialogue with God as a single entity, yet still had dialogue with each other for purposes of refinement.

Towards the end of my final year at college the verses/words were still in the main answers to the earlier thoughts and (private) prayers of both of us, that is, an attenuated and at times obscure dialogue. It was during that summer that I discontinued the journal, and I did this for two reasons. Firstly, there were the time pressures resulting from an increased work load during this, my final year at college, as exams and a lengthy dissertation had to be 'shoe horned' into the limited time available. More significantly, however, there was the sheer scale of the record, as journal entries for a single day could now number six to seven, with a paragraph allocated to each. It turned out that from this point forward and particularly following a much needed holiday in Turkey, that the nature of the dialogue with God began to change.

1,2—Testing, Testing!

Dining out in the evening had played a central role in Chris's agonisingly slow recovery from anorexia, and it had remained our practice to go to the local pub in the early evening, even though we didn't always eat there any more. One such evening, during the January of my final semester at college was particularly memorable. In the pub, we discussed how the LORD talked to us, that is, Chris, myself, and the LORD in normal person to person conversation, as if there were three (or should that be five?) people in the room, and I wondered why He did that. I was doubting now, doubting the validity of all the verses we were receiving, and especially so, because the content of what was being communicated had undergone a marked change. A terrible, terrible story was emerging from amongst the apocalypticism, idiom, and hyperbole of the verses, a story of dreadful, impending action upon an unsuspecting world. We were learning that the Old Testament God, who for so long had been neatly pigeon-holed by Christians into the box marked 'old covenant' was alive, well, and very active. Just one year away from the celebrations planned to mark the end of the millennium, the picture began to emerge of an impending 'Day of the LORD.' As the end of the century approached, I had visions of donning a sandwich board bearing the traditional legend, 'repent, repent for the end of the world is nigh!' But I wasn't sceptical so much as mystified as to why we should be privy to this knowledge, indeed why did He bother with us in this way at all, it didn't seem to happen to other Christians?

In the past my doubts about these verses had often been answered with the reply of 2 Timothy 3:16, and this had usually sufficed. This time, however, as we sat beer in hand in front of the pub fire, I was prayerfully asking a different and very personal question. The LORD had never lost his patience with my testing questions, and it seemed at times as if doubt was the very engine of faith. Indeed, I have always thought of doubt as the residual carbon dioxide permanently present in the lungs, which provides the essential stimulus needed to enable us to draw further breaths (of faith?). I suppose my question could be reduced to a succinct, why us? In response, Chris *immediately* received one of the now rare New Testament verses—1 John 2:14 which reads:

> I write to you, fathers, because you have known him who is from the beginning. I write to you, young men, because you are strong, and the word of God lives in you, and you have overcome the evil one.

Now it may be objected that this verse is written, as opposed to being spoken, and that it was written to two groups of recipients—fathers and young men. In a sense, we classified as both these latter—being both heads of house and comparatively new or 'young' Christians. But in any case such objections are *non-sequiturs*, if only because the verse/word must be placed into the contemporary context of the immediately preceding prayerful enquiry.

The awesome essence of the word lies in its affirmation of what a Christian *is*, and it is this affirmation that was given as the answer to that enquiry. A Christian is one who knows (not just knows of) God, one who is in a constant, communicative relationship with him, and within whom the word of God (Jesus) lives. The reply was consequently profound in the extreme, and in paraphrase may be restated: "Your ongoing (prophetic) experience results from your personal relationship with me, and is (or should be), the normal experience of all Christians, within whom God makes his home."

Small Groups

From the earliest days of our Christian walk we had been aware of the small group model of church, as exemplified by the cell structure of the Korean Church—the biggest single church in the world. This awareness had been via a member of that first healing prayer group, whose avid reading of Christian material had introduced her, and subsequently us, to this (new?) way of being church. But if 'the proof of the pudding is in the eating' then we both found from personal experience, that being part of a small prayer group gave a greater sense of the presence of God, than any conventional church service—whatever the denomination. In Chris's case the presence of God, or more particularly the peace of God had always been the reason for her involvement with small groups, providing as it did a salve for her anxiety, which the drugs failed to alleviate. It was the prospect of this peace, which induced her to continue to participate, time and time again. As a theology student I found that this raised a number of questions, not the least of which was whether this format in which I felt closest to God, reflected the structure of the earliest churches. It is certainly true to say that a (typical?) British congregation numbering perhaps one hundred and fifty, has little in common with the normal Pauline assemblies whose numbers rarely exceeded thirty—the capacity of a typical 'house church' (Philemon 2).

This dissimilarity between the modern church worship meetings and those early groups prompts a number of other questions, which have to do with composition. Typically, modern services can include people at all stages in their Christian walk, ranging from catechumens (novices) to mature believers. In a societal context where 'things spiritual' are so poorly understood, this can be an imperfect means of communicating the Christian faith to the 'seeker.' Thus the modern church leader—who is invariably a pastor/preacher—tends to be constrained by this factor, which when combined with the directive 'to proclaim the gospel,' leaves little room for flexibility in what transpires. There are two conventional ways of dealing with this problem. Firstly, one can try to aim or direct the services towards one particular group or another, but this is difficult unless the church membership as a whole endeavors to ensure in advance, that the target group is present in the building. The second and arguably complimentary solution is to hold meetings at other times during the week, which are directed towards specific groups. Home fellowship and alpha course groups are the two types of meeting which come to mind here, but are often biased towards the communication of factual information about Christianity, as distinct from communicating Christ. The communication of Christ, it seems, is all too often left to smaller, *ad hoc* groupings of like minded Christians, who organize themselves into prayer couplets, triplets, and larger groups.

One advantage held by the small group over the larger meeting has to do with the embarrassment factor. In a small group it is often possible to exhibit certain forms of experiential behavior, which would be deemed unacceptable in the normal Sunday morning meeting. Personal experience of the presence of God can take many physical forms, which can go far beyond the very personal and subjective 'tingling' reported by many Christians. One may cite for example barking and whooping—behavior considered to be beyond the pale at most services, and probably in most small groups for that matter, but the essential point is that consensus is likely to be more easily achieved amongst a small number of like minded persons. In this regard, I well remember a church delegation walking out of a large Bible Week praise meeting because of the actions of the speaker, whose experience of the Holy Spirit was worked out behaviorally (at the lectern) as a series of body spasms and convulsions. I too, felt ill at ease with this manifestation, until that is, I (much) later experienced this same phenomenon myself during a prayer session within a small group. The point to be emphasized here is that the inhibition threshold of mutually acceptable behavior is much lower for smaller groups, than it is for larger ones because of the wider disparity in the makeup of that larger group. There seems to be some evidence in the Pauline letters (1 Cor. 11:20; Rom. 16:23) that individual house churches met together, on occasion, in a larger gathering at which the 'uninstructed' could be present. It is at this larger, more public gathering that Paul prohibits (1 Cor. 14:20–28) the corporate use of uninterpreted tongues, but is there an inference here that this prohibition might not have applied to the smaller, constituent house churches? This issue of tongues still remains controversial today, and exemplifies the problems inherent in holding larger meetings that are accessible to the (uninstructed) public.

On this analysis, it seems that there is a strong argument for laying greater (if not the greatest) emphasis on small groups within the Church, as one means of ensuring the (spiritual) growth of the more mature Christians.

It had always seemed to me that the desired and intended outcome of a Sunday morning service—to meet with God—is never achieved to the same extent, as it is within a small group. The problem is not that modern services are unwieldy due to size, or that the liturgy gets in the way, or even that the 'rational' or 'cerebral' element of a modern service suffocates the presence of God. Instead, it has much more to do with the fact that for mature Christians, it simply isn't 'where the (main) action is.' Over the years I have been involved with several small prayer groups, and irrespective of the intention or purpose for which they were formed, the outcome is always the same, that is, growth in fellowship with God and with each other. Almost without exception the intended topic for a session was 'hijacked' by the LORD, to be replaced with a different priority, which invariably results in the development of the groups' collective abilities in prayer and prophecy. In short, most of the time was given over to the enhancement of (spiritual) communication skills, so much so, that I now believe this to have been the principal aim all along. Fellowship with God must be the prime directive for Christians, and is one facet of righteousness (maintained relationship with God), and righteousness, which is served by communication with God, must not be neglected for fear of being accused of hiding in a 'holy huddle.' On the contrary, it is difficult (not impossible however!) to serve God without first finding out what He wants, and that requires dialogical communication during time spent in his company. Once this is achieved, it may come as a complete surprise to find out just how light (Matt. 11:30) his burden actually is!

In practice, each prayer group session would tend to produce a composite word, or prayer to pray as its outcome, and I began to wonder how much this mirrors the ancient church. Certainly Paul's letter to the Romans would have been passed around the house churches of Romans 16, and the practice of prophecy is shown to be a corporate activity in Romans 12:6 by the use of the second person plural.[1] Prophecy, along with ministering or service, is singled out from amongst the 'gifts' discussed here, as a corporate activity, with the remainder depicted as the province of individuals. In light of this the question which must be asked is: does modern prophecy—as occasionally observed in some Sunday services—mirror that which took place in the ancient church? In answer to this, it must be immediately acknowledged that modern prophecy can by no means be described as a corporate activity, and invariably consists of a single utterance by one individual. Although without doubt the oracle given is of God, one is left wondering

---

1. This is somewhat obscured in the more modern translations of the bible, but see the King James Version.

whether a richer experience could be achieved, if at that point, the congregation abandoned what they were doing, and switched to praying their responses to the given word? Would further words be given, I wonder? It appears that modern Christian prophecy, at least as seen in Sunday services, more properly mirrors the *perceived* activities of the lone Old Testament prophet, rather than a post Pentecost New Testament model. Perhaps our ideas of what it meant to be a prophet in Bible times are in need drastic revision.

11

Prophecy—The Old Testament Model

SOMETIME AROUND THE BEGINNING of my final semester at college, the slow realisation that Chris's facility was in some way a 'prophetic' gifting was beginning to 'crystallize' in my mind. I believe that although this realisation was contributed to by the college course, it did not seem to be a conscious process achieved through any of the lecture or study materials. Moreover, the *Prophets* module itself was—apart from some very insightful questions in the introduction—essentially a catalogue of the role and activities of the Old Testament prophets, within the social and political contexts of their time. Some of those introductory questions certainly fired my imagination and many remain to irk me still, but I knew that there was no possibility of addressing them on an undergraduate course. Besides, I felt (misguidedly as it turned out) that my interests lay elsewhere, and in the frantic push to complete dissertations and swot up for exams, I was not in any position to coalesce my studies and personal experiences, into a final, condensed essence.

Amongst those questions, lay issues concerning the ancient near eastern provenance of the Old Testament prophets, in particular, how closely did their practice mirror the practices of the prophets of their pagan neighbors? Certainly, in terms of lifestyle (hateful word!), mindset, and worldview, the Israelites had much in common with the neighboring nations, raising the possibility of shared prophetic practices. Then there was the minefield of etymology, that is, the study of the meanings of the original (Hebrew) words and their ancient near eastern counterparts. As noted earlier, the synchronic meaning (the meaning of a word at the time) can only be determined from its context, and this too threw up further questions. The word for prophet (*nabi*) is itself an intriguing case in point, where the lost, Hebrew verbal root has been related to the terms, 'to boil up,' or 'to bubble forth.' But precisely what is bubbling and boiling here? Does this term refer to the animation of the prophet in his act of utterance to an audience, or does it describe his *reception* of a word from God—an essentially internal process within the prophet? Only context can (hopefully) decide.

When one pursues the etymology further, by examining languages cognate with Hebrew, one finds that in the old Akkadian—a precursor of the Aramaic of New Testament Galilee—the word for prophet has been translated as "one who is called." Such an interpretation is without doubt supportive of our own contemporary understanding of what a prophet is, and the much later Arabic word meaning "to proclaim or announce" further reinforces this. But alternative explanations of the Akkadian cognate verb *nabû(m)*, based on actual usage of the word in everyday life, indicate that it can have the meaning, 'to name,' or 'to call upon.' A common or shared interpretation of the Hebrew (*nabi*) and the Akkadian (*nabû(m)*) would indicate a non-proclamatory role by humans, in which they were primarily identified as ones who called upon or invoked the gods. Quite apart from placing the initiative in the divine-human relationship in the hands of the prophet, this interpretation is capable of supporting the view that it is the *internal* experience of God that defines the prophetic encounter, and hence what it means to be a prophet. To call upon, invoke or *summon up* an internal voice was the common practice of all prophets in the ancient near east, but the question remains as to whether it was the practice of Israelite prophets to summon up The Internal Voice? Scholars, however, consider the etymology alone to be a weak argument, which must be supported by other evidence.

The 'Conventional' Prophet

What is a prophet? It is fairly certain that if one were to ask the average person this question, the answer coming back would be a biblical character who has the capacity to foretell the future. Therefore in the secular understanding the 'conventional' prophet is a man (almost always a man!) who although able to predict the future almost certainly ceased to exist in the mists of biblical time. Indeed, his function in modern, Western society appears to have been assumed by the tabloid astrologer! When asked this same question the average, modern Christian fairs little better, save to say that in addition to foretelling the future, the prophet is understood to be one who speaks God's words to the modern church—either to specific local churches or to the church in its full catholic sense. In both senses the prophet's function is therefore essentially oracular, and in the latter, catholic sense prominent churchmen may be deemed 'prophetic' during the giving of sermons or indeed any other public speaking. Modern prophecy as it is understood in a 'charismatic' setting is likewise oracular, with the prophet receiving and announcing God's word to the assembled people of God (church), and this dual activity is perceived to be simultaneous. The 'charismatic' churches normally consider the prophet to be a single person—usually a man, who is stereotypically perceived to be some kind of latter day derivative of the Old Testament prophet. Such churches seem to see their prophets (and there are precious few of these) as rather odd individuals, who stand in direct line of succession to the animal skin clad and leather-belted individuals of old Israel. Moreover, this perception doesn't appear to have been mitigated in any way by two thousand years of Christianity, but then why should it, if the first Christians themselves closely identified their own prophets with those of the Old Testament? It has always been assumed that it was the oracular nature of prophecy, which linked the sophisticated, urban Christians of Paul's letters, with the rough, itinerant, prophets of the historical books of the bible, or the prophets of the prophetic canon, but was that really the case? Is there a more fundamental factor that identifies a man or woman as a prophet?

When I questioned Chris closely about her own experience of receiving verses and words from the LORD, I began to notice that it exactly paralleled one suggested Hebrew root meaning of prophet (to boil up, to bubble forth). Now clearly these latter expressions are verbal metaphors, which if correct, liken the prophet's 'activity' to the physical action described. It would therefore, be easy to see how this could be construed as the act of giving an oracle, in which a very animated and ecstatic prophet 'frothed out' his word to an audience. But, if we were to credit the ancient Hebrews with considerably more observational skills, then the metaphor becomes capable of describing the prophet's inner experience, an experience more closely akin to that of Chris. Close observation of boiling water can reveal much, and the physics of the process tells us that minute bubbles of water vapor are formed when the SVP (saturated vapor pressure) of the liquid rises to equal the atmospheric pressure. Heating the water causes bubbles to appear from nowhere deep in the body of the liquid, which then rise to break through the surface, that is, the boundary or interface separating the two phases—water and air, and then they completely disappear again. For as long as men (women?) have boiled pots of water, this observation would not have been lost on the sharp eyed.

There is, however, another barrel to this double-barrelled metaphor—if my use of a metaphor to describe a metaphor can be forgiven, and that concerns the second expression 'to bubble forth.' The Judean hills surrounding Jerusalem are made of porous limestone—a fact that king David turned to his great advantage when he captured the Jebusite stronghold (2 Sam. 5:8). Water falls on these hills as the early (spring) and late (autumn) rains, and percolates down through the rock gradually dissolving small amounts of limestone (calcium carbonate) as it does so. In the hot, dry summer between these falls of rain, life, both human and animal, depends upon retrieving water from the wells, pools, and cisterns that are fed by underground springs issuing from fault lines in the rocks. Throughout the summer this water would lie in the pools, and would be mildly alkaline (pH 8.3) due to the dissolved carbonate. Excess, mildly acidic rainwater (pH 5.6) falling in the autumn and entering the pools as groundwater run off, would react with the lying water to produce gaseous carbon dioxide, as a result of driving the following equilibrium to the left:

$$CO_{2(aq)} + 2H_2O_{(l)} \rightleftharpoons HCO_{3\ (aq)}^{-} + H_3O^{+}_{(aq)}$$

Under certain circumstances the emission of gaseous carbon dioxide would be seen as minute bubbles pin-pricking the water surface, similar in fact, to the tiny bubbles observed in boiling water.

But how, it may be asked, does the observation of the behavior of bubbles—used as a metaphor—relate to the internal prophetic process? The answer lies in visualising the Word of God as a bubble that emerges from an indefinable nowhere, which is as deep inside the prophet, as the bubble is within the water. The Word of God, whether 'visually' or 'audibly' received appears suddenly at the surface (of the mind) having crossed the divine-human, consciousness interface, just as the bubble crosses the water/air phase boundary. Water, understood as being virtually synonymous with life itself, would represent the divine 'phase' of such an interface, with air being the human 'phase.' Both metaphorical phases are of course part of the same system, and occupy the same dimensions of space and time, that is, the prophet himself! Moreover, the essence of the action is quickness, for just as the bubbles pop up quickly—intruding almost—into the air, so the Word pops up into conscious awareness, and something that was not there, suddenly appears or surfaces. Interestingly, the phase boundary between water and air is only a weak boundary known as the 'surface tension'—a line of water molecules held in place by the neighboring (underlying) molecules. This barrier, which is a barrier yet not a barrier, permits many things to cross it in both directions, and its metaphorical use in this way should warn us not to under value the observational skills of a past (unscientific?) age. Much of the foregoing might seem conjecture based upon an obscure etymology, yet strangely, support for the idea may be found at the boundaries of modern psychology. Indeed, the process just described may be labelled *transliminality* where this term has been defined by Thalbourne and his colleagues as a "susceptibility to, and awareness of, large volumes of imagery, ideation, and affect—these phenomena being generated by subliminal, supraliminal, and/or external input." Transliminality describes the extent to which paranormal belief and experience, magical ideation, manic experience, creative personality, and mystical experience cross the threshold of the mind—a barrier that is simply more permeable in some people than it is in others.

If it is true to say that the (bubble) metaphor is describing an internal process within the prophet, and as a result, causing the prophet to be identified as one who has this 'activity' going on inside him, then it follows that our (modern?) concept of the prophet as merely an oracle giver could be wrong. Rather, on this analysis, the single most important factor identifying a prophet is a (communicating) relationship with God! Indeed, the church may be looking in entirely the wrong direction in its attempts to identify prophets, who are not often seen to be the weakest, most unassuming members of the church. Moreover, much of what is communicated to the prophet in his divine encounters may *not* be for announcement to the church at large, for in any communicating relationship there are matters that are *privy* to that relationship.

The stimulation of my thinking in this way about what it is to be a prophet was, as noted earlier, the result of my questioning Chris about her own internal experience. The receipt of a verse, e.g. 2 Samuel 23:2, would come as a 'pop in' or an intrusion, initially interrupting her own thoughts with the single word, 'two.' Compelled to address the intrusion, she would ask the question 'two what?' in her mind, before receiving the full verse 2 Samuel 23: 'two' in reply. Most verses given would be variations on this theme. Although not prophetically gifted to anything like the same extent as Chris, I too have experienced this same intrusion into my thoughts. By way of example, I can cite one particularly uneventful 'quiet time,' when I was praying to Jesus along the lines of: "you are my LORD, friend, master teacher etc. etc." As a creature of habit, I had prayed this rather boring list of Jesus' relational roles towards me many, many times before, usually, sad to say, with my mind in neutral. Imagine then, my surprise when I found myself sleepily (this was very early in the morning!) speaking out another word in the middle of this listing of roles—the word 'servant.' I nearly fell off the chair! "You can't be serious," I said, somewhat like a famous tennis player of yesteryear, as the full realisation of the implied simile with Peter (John 13:8) dawned on me! The LORD definitely has a way of getting one's attention, and the word 'intrusion' just about sums it up!

A Common Factor?

In perfect hindsight I can now see how laboriously slowly we were progressing, in this very personal walk with God. It had taken the LORD a number of years to get us praying together as *the* norm, and our dialogue with him had remained attenuated—despite being much more informed—as the final year at college concluded. Summer arrived and with exams behind me, we jetted off to spend a relaxing two weeks in the Turkish sun, or at least that was our intention. Now whilst I like hot weather (and this was very, very hot!) neither my body, which erupts into heat spots, nor Chris have a similar penchant for the sun, and this occasion was further complicated by Chris's apparent allergic reaction to the local Turkish beer! Indeed, within two beers of our arrival, Chris's feet and ankles had swollen into huge red blotches from toe to sock line, and for the next seven days we found we were virtually prisoners in our apartment. We purchased antihistamines from a very helpful, English-speaking pharmacist, and a local English restaurateur recommended that Chris bathe her feet in vinegar. After buying the vinegar at the local grocer's shop, Chris was from that day forward known as 'the vinegar lady' by the local Turks! The net effect of all this was that we were 'grounded' for a week. We couldn't even reach the nearest bus stop, and apart from meals at a nearby café—a painful two hundred yards distant—we were compelled to spend the week in the apartment complex.

The whole week was spent in a kind of sensory deprivation, because quite naturally the talk around us was in Turkish, whether on TV or radio, or amongst the apartment staff. We had little to do with the other English guests, since they usually spent the whole day sunbathing by the pool, and the sunshine made Chris's painful feet worse, forcing her to remain indoors. The planned excursions to Ephesus and Capadocia were abandoned, and we settled down to a sedentary holiday pace revolving around mealtimes and drinks from the pool bar. Circumstances, it seemed, had conspired to provide us with a very extended period without activity—a long and very relaxed period akin to our evening sojourns in the pub back in England, and the verses came in like manner to those times in the pub. This time, however, the attenuation that had previously been a feature of our dialogue with the LORD was missing, and we found that the number of verses increased exponentially, often in storyline sequences of three or four and in response to our prayerful questions. During that week, Chris reached another milestone in her recovery, as oppression—spiritual oppression, which had hitherto been superimposed on her depression was lifted by the LORD's direct action. Although she continued to be clinically depressed and would again plumb the suicidal depths it was as if a black cloud had been lifted from over her head. Strangely, on the afternoon that this happened we were both affected by a rapturous euphoria, the like of which we have not known either before or since, and which continued until the following day. Another lasting outcome of the holiday was to be our avowed intention to maintain this close, intimate, and now immediate dialogue with the LORD. From this point forward, we devoted an hour or two of subsequent Sunday afternoons to a relaxed, extended meal spent solely in the LORD's company, and exclusively for the purposes of dialogue.

Upon our return from holiday, we maintained our intention to spend regular, joint sessions with the LORD, but although I knew that this 'conversation' with God was 'kosher,' I needed to know where it could be found and validated from within scripture. Thus I began a long and still continuing process of personal research into the phenomenon of prophecy, as it is depicted in the Old Testament. I was able to establish, at least to my own satisfaction, that it was the prophets' own internal experience of God which marked them out as such. This, it seems, is the common factor which they shared with Chris, and which they presumably share with many others. But what precisely brings people into relationship with God in this very intimate way? Certainly, oracles are not common to all those described as prophets, since the Hebrew term for a prophet, (*nabi*), first appears in Genesis 20:7 where it is applied to Abraham, and the question which must be asked of this verse is: Why should king Abimelech venerate Abraham as a 'prophet' when, as an oracle giver, he fails to qualify? It seems that in Abraham's case the key word is 'friend,' since Abraham was God's friend or special favorite and this is certainly R K Harrison's interpretation of the designation 'prophet.' Perhaps it is the desire for a trusting, friendship relationship, which is the single, most important feature of the prophet's life, and that which is common to all prophets, whether Old Testament, New Testament or indeed contemporary. The outward and visible sign of any friendship is time spent in each others company, and this is principally exemplified by conversation, and where one of the parties is a spiritual entity (God) this is likely to be an internal experience.

Prophecy—The Scriptural Emphasis

If, as I have been advocating, the emphasis should be placed on the dialogical aspects of prophecy rather than on its oracular out workings, how then is dialogue or conversation with God arrived at? What are the 'mechanics' of the process, and exactly what is involved in the 'raising up' of a prophet? In our own case we were left in no doubt that this process involved affliction, and that it was the LORD himself who had 'afflicted' us all through the early years of Chris's illness. Those years included seven years as committed Christians, during which Chris suffered from deep depression, indeed often suicidal depression. Faced with such daily suffering, we were prompted to give ongoing and serious consideration to our relationship with the God who *admitted* that He was responsible for it, and yet who at one and the same time showed us great and repeated kindnesses. Equally, we were left in no doubt about precisely when the affliction ended, that is, during the first week of the Turkish holiday, with the lifting of the oppression. The (instant) lifting of the oppression coincided exactly with the commencement of the full and immediate phase in our dialogical relationship with the LORD, who from that point forward continually stressed that *He* no longer afflicted us. Our own experience of the 'prophetic process,' if true, immediately throws up a number of new questions concerning (clinical) depression. In particular, is affliction with depression—a known phenomenon amongst the Old Testament prophets—the necessary precursor to dialogue with God, and thereby essential to the 'raising up' of a prophet? As a theology graduate, I was and remain, consumed with curiosity about whether this can be demonstrated from the scriptures.

12

Depression In The Old Testament

I HAVE MADE REFERENCE to the book of Jonah on several occasions, drawing attention to the fact that Jonah, the man, exhibited symptoms of clinical depression, and it has long been recognized that depression was a factor in the lives of the Old Testament prophets. From a purely medical standpoint, depression can be differentiated into three main categories the first of which is termed 'minor depression,' where the condition is considered mild, difficult to diagnose and is often obscured by a number of physical (psychosomatic) complaints. In 'major depression,' however, the presentation includes hopelessness and helplessness and is qualitatively distinct, that is, not merely a state of 'sadness.' There is, moreover, a continuum within which it is not possible to draw a sharp line between 'sadness,' suffering from low mood or depression, and being 'clinically depressed.' A small percentage of sufferers extend this continuum into a third and final psychotic stage of depression in which they can present with the more severe symptoms of depressive stupor, severe agitation, suicidal intent and/or delusions. Some of these recognized, medical indicators of depression are present in the scriptures, but only where two, or preferably more than two are present together in a text, is it safe to conclude that the prophet concerned is depressed. But how can these indicators—usually described in modern medical language—be identified within what is essentially Hebrew prose and poetry? In short, how is depression subjectively illustrated in those passages of the Old Testament that refer to the prophets?

Depression Motifs in the Old Testament

Suicide, suicidal intent or 'suicidality' clearly feature amongst the motifs or markers of depression found in certain passages of the Old Testament, where they might better be described as a desire not to live. Suicidality is an indicator of the most extreme, (often psychotic) stage of depression, and where self-harm is expressed within the scriptures, it may be clearly understood to point to severe depression of which it is a primary identifier or 'marker'. This 'suicidality' marker labels Moses (Ex. 32:32; Num. 11:15), Elijah (1 Kings 19:4) and Jonah (Jonah 4:3, 8–9) as fellow sufferers from depression, and it is interesting that they each share the same sentiment when expressing their suicidal desires. Moses expresses that desire by asking the LORD to "blot me out of the book that you have written" (Ex. 32:32), or to "put me to death at once" (Num. 11:15), whilst Elijah implores, "O LORD, take away my life" (1 Kings 19:4). In similar vein to Elijah, Jonah petitions, "O LORD, please take my life from me" (Jonah 4:3). The common theme here is not so much that these prophets want to die, as that they would rather *not live*, and it has been noted in modern studies that this is very different from an active, energetic desire to destroy oneself. Indeed, this feature is a stereotypical identifier of modern depressives, who rarely have the energy to kill themselves—although sadly many do succeed.

Anger is also a noticeably prevalent feature in the lives of two of the prophets, namely Jonah (Jonah 4:1, 4, 9) and significantly Moses (Ex. 11:8; 16:20; 32:19,22; Lev. 10:16; & Num. 16:15; 31:14). The three references to anger in Jonah 4 lie closely associated with three references to the desire for self-harm (Jonah 4:3, 8–9), the quintessential depression 'marker,' and so reinforce a diagnosis of depression in Jonah's case. With Moses the situation is a little less certain, since the two depression markers (suicidality and anger) are not as closely associated with each other. The more numerous references to Moses' anger do not seem for the most part to be explicitly in situations where the prophet is otherwise identified as depressed. But Moses does, nevertheless, exhibit suicidal desires (Ex. 32:32; Num. 11:15), and he seems likely to have suffered from repressed anger for much of the time, which erupted during particularly stressful moments as a symptom of chronic, low-grade depression. In Exodus 32, anger and 'suicidality' both mark Moses' depression following a fast. Poor self-worth or excessive humility is another depression marker or motif found in certain passages of the Old Testament, and like "recurrent thoughts of death," it is another of the diagnostic criteria for a major depressive episode listed in the "Diagnostic and Statistical Manual of Mental Disorders" published by the American Psychiatric Association. One of those Old Testament passages recounts the story of (soon to be king) Saul, who although never directly described as a prophet, certainly seems to have caused debate on the matter amongst those who knew him (1 Sam. 10:11). The disparity between the young, powerful, and fit individual introduced at the beginning of 1 Samuel 9 and his own opinion of himself as the insecure, overly-humble, and self-deprecating Saul of 1 Samuel 9:21 can only be explained in terms of depression. In similar vein, this feature of inappropriate and excessive humility is found on the lips of the prophet, Elijah, in his petition to the LORD in 1 Kings 19:4, and immediately following his request to die.

It is certainly the case that the Elijah narratives contain a number of oblique connections with depression, and the first indication concerning Elijah's mental state comes at the beginning of 1 Kings 18 where we learn that he left Zarephath in Sidon on the LORD's instruction going into Samaria where 'the famine was severe' (1 Kgs 18:2). It would therefore not be reading too much into the text to say that Elijah—in common with most of his compatriots—was in a state of semi-starvation just prior to the Mt. Carmel contest, since arranging for the assembly of (the leaders of) "all Israel" at Mt. Carmel would inevitably take days, if not weeks, to accomplish. Unfortunately, the reader is not told how long it took to assemble "all Israel" and Elijah's semi-starved condition would remain conjecture but for 1 Kings 18:46 where the text records Elijah running in front of Ahab's chariot. The latter verse has almost always been taken to indicate that this abnormal feat was a function of Elijah's triumphant, elation—the direct result of 'his' victory over the prophets of Baal. Such 'hyperactivity' can, however, be interpreted very differently. Experiments with animals (rodents) have indicated that food restriction (semi-starvation) induces hyperactivity, which in the case of rats is observed as a rapid increase in their running activity. This is entirely consistent with the behavior of some anorectics—held under Mental Health Act Section in tertiary care units—who remorselessly pace the floor for hours on end. It must be emphasized, however, that animal models are not directly relevant to human beings, and although not all anorectics are hyperactive it does appear that semi-starvation produces two effects in some humans. Semi-starvation stimulates serotonin turnover (catabolism) whilst secondly stimulating hyperactivity, with the latter result enhancing the former. Put simply, it would seem that hyperactivity further depletes the already reduced serotonin levels in the hypothalamus, brought about by semi-starvation. Significantly, this exacerbation of serotonin deficit through semi-starvation—which as noted earlier can be correlated with severe depression—is being presented to the reader in the form of the hyperactivity described at the end of 1 Kings 18.

The full significance of this glimpse into Elijah's mental state at the end of chapter 18 does not become apparent until the structure of the following chapter is discerned. I have examined the structure of 1 Kings 19:2-21 elsewhere and have been able to determine that the text breaks down into four discrete periods of speech/action (19:2b-4; 5b-6d; 7-9a; 9c-21) separated from each other by three equally discrete punctuations of sleep (19:5a; 6e; 9b). The first period of speech/action is the second longest of the four, and the remaining three periods increase progressively in length with the final period being the longest of all. Interestingly, the intervening sleep periods appear to show a gradation in depth of sleep as represented by the Hebrew terms used, since in v. 5a Elijah both lies down and sleeps whereas in v. 6e he only lies down, and in v. 9b he merely 'lodges' in the cave. The Hebrew term translated as 'lodge' or 'spend the night' is in addition indicating a much increased *duration* for the shallower sleep period of v. 9b. The spatial relationship between the sections of speech/action and the intervening sleep periods in 1 Kings 19:2-21 is easier to see if it is represented graphically. Clearly, the text does not provide any numerical information and therefore it is impossible to draw such a structure to 'scale.' Accordingly, the sleep architecture between the speech/action and sleep sequences are drawn in broken line to indicate this absence of this information, and the verses are shown numbered and lettered according to the punctuation shown in the NRSV, that is, in phrases:

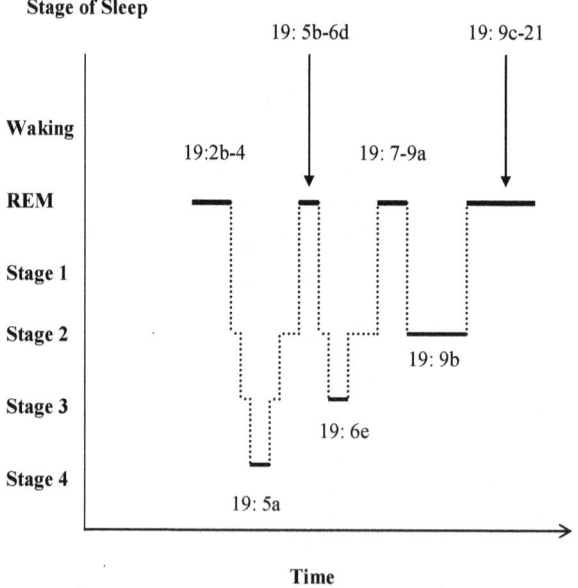

Fig. 1   'Derived Etic' Hypnogram of 1 Kings 19:2-21

The structure produced in this way is recognisable as that of a *hypnogram*—the technical term used in sleep research for the graphical record of a night's sleep, and the speech/action periods of 1 Kings 19 can be seen to correspond directly to Rapid Eye Movement (REM) or dreaming sleep. But this is *not* the sleep pattern of a normal, healthy adult, which typically undergoes deformation during depression such that the duration of the first REM/dreaming period will elongate from about 3 minutes in the normal young adult to perhaps 20 minutes in depressives. Typically, the first REM period of a depressive accounts for perhaps 25% of total REM/dreaming sleep across the night leaving the remaining periods of dreaming sleep proportionately reduced in length, yet still maintaining a progressive increase in duration. It is this pattern of an extended/lengthened first dream *relative* to the length of those following that is displayed in 1 Kings 19. The speech/action sequences of chapter 19 are in reality the dreams of a very depressed Elijah, perhaps the logical outcome of the psychophysiological condition that appears to have finally overwhelmed him at the end of chapter 18. The probability that such a (speech/action) sleep pattern could have been transmitted accidentally or randomly is in excess of a million to 1. In order to emphasize the intentional (non random) nature of this pattern the author/editor ingeniously places the two other depression motifs (excessive worthlessness and 'suicidality') within the content of the first, elongated dream period of the hypnogram (1 Kgs 19:2b–4), a feature, which as we have seen is *characteristic* for depressive dreaming. To centre two depression motifs within a third such motif would suggest a deliberate and knowledgeable authorial/editorial intent to record the relationship between depression and the onset of altered state, spiritual encounter. Such knowledge goes some considerable way beyond the mere observation, reinforcement, and recording of culturally significant patterns of prophetic, nocturnal behavior.

Depression, Dreaming, and Meditation

At this stage we might ask why it is important to know that Elijah and the prophets were depressed? Indeed, why should we be surprised when we find that virtually the whole of 1 Kings 19 is a sequence of dreams, given that scripture (Deut. 13:1, 3, 5 KJV) appears to use the terms 'prophet' and 'dreamer of dreams' interchangeably? One answer based on sleep research lies in Hobson's understanding of major depression as "a functional disorder of the very same neuronal systems that control dreaming," which could mean that "to be prone to depression is to be prone to REM sleep (dreaming) and vice versa." The principle neuronal system involved in both depression and dreaming has been acknowledged to be the serotonergic system, and both depression and dreaming are said to involve conditions of serotonin deficit in the brain. But this doesn't appear to get us much further on if the dreaming concerned is about trivial, personal or everyday issues, which the dreamer often, indeed typically, fails to remember. There must be some other factor which induces the depressed dreamer to dream dreams that firstly reflect important, universal, moral themes, and secondly permit a better recall of a significantly increased amount of dream content. Expressed differently, what changes the universal, human experience of dreaming into an altered state of consciousness that promotes access to the Deity? In short, what differentiates the unremarkable, personal dream from an encounter with God?

In order to answer this question it might prove illuminating to look at another altered state of consciousness—meditation, for on examination meditation is found to exhibit certain features that it shares with dreaming. The first point of similarity—according to Murphy and Donovan's comprehensive review of meditation research—lies in the fact that there is "evidence to support the hypothesis that TM (transcendental meditation) is associated with acutely reduced hypothalamic and peripheral serotonergic activity." Thus, it may be said that meditation states share the same underlying serotonin deficit condition as depression/dreaming, and interaction with serotonin is moreover a feature of LSD intoxication—the recreational drug of choice of the 1960s and 70s. Secondly, it may be noted that all three of these altered states (dreaming, meditation, and LSD intoxication) involve the phenomenon known as synesthesia or cross modality perception. Synesthesia has been described by Goodman as the "transmutation of sensory modalities, where sound may be seen or color experienced by the sense of smell and so on." This is a common feature of a number of 'prophetic' texts in the Old Testament (1 Sam. 3:1; 2 Sam. 7:17) where the "Word of the LORD" is received within a dream or vision state, that is, it is *seen*, as in Exodus 20:18 where the Hebrew records that "all the people *saw* the voices." There is, however, an important distinction between the various meditative states and either depression/dreaming or LSD intoxication, since it may be said that meditative states, like those of shamanic trance, require some level of *intellectual commitment* in order to succumb to them. Put simply, this may amount to the will or desire to enter such a state with the intention of seeking encounter with God within it. What all this suggests is that determined meditative practice taking place immediately before a night's dreaming may—on the basis that dreaming and meditation share the same brain chemistry—direct that dreaming in terms of both meaningful content and completeness of dream recall.

Meaningful content in a scriptural context must mean contact with God following meditation, and the question that now arises is: Can scripture provide an example of such meditative preparation prior to dreaming? I believe that the answer is to be found once again in that strange and apparently motiveless verse at the end of 1 Kings 18 where Elijah runs the eighteen miles from Mount Carmel to Jezreel ahead of Ahab's chariot. We have already examined this verse and found evidence from modern physiological studies that the hyperactive running activity is related to semi-starvation, and involves significantly altered brain chemistry consistent with depression/dreaming. But the verse also tells us that "the hand of the LORD was on Elijah" (NRSV), which is a shorthand, Hebrew way of saying that Elijah was under the power/control of the Spirit of God. This is important in as much as we find evidence in other pre-modern cultures of this same kind of spirit-controlled running. David-Neel in her much reproduced "Magic and Mystery in Tibet" records parallel behavior by the lamas of Tibet who engage in *lung gom pa* running. These runners are able to cover immense distances in a swift, leaping gait whilst alone and in a quiet, altered state of consciousness, and David-Neel affirms that such 'trance' runs are *meditative* states that cannot be interrupted. This may well be at the root of Obadiah's worries about Elijah earlier on in the chapter (1 Kgs 18:12) where he expresses the fear: "As soon as I have gone from you, the spirit of the LORD will carry you I know not where." Elijah's behavior is to be expected from a cross-cultural perspective, as well as from the biomedical data on semi-starvation we looked at earlier, and is the meditative forerunner to the meaningful dreams of the following chapter.

Returning briefly to our own situation it will be remembered that Chris was in the habit of meditating, but it has to be said that she did not experience, or at least recall, any meaningful dreams. This may be simply due to the fact that her meditations were often of short duration, or possibly because her meditative techniques were not as exhaustive as those of oriental origin. Certainly, her sleep pattern was very disturbed and it is the case that antidepressants of whatever variety (Tricyclics, MAOIs, SSRIs etc.) are known to interfere (understandably) with the characteristic, depressive hypnogram. Nevertheless, it seems clear that the practice of meditation when at the service of an intellectual resolve to contact the Deity can still serve the people of God well.

The Prophet Making Process—Jonah

In the previous sections I have noted, in what I hope has not been too technical a manner the various indicators of depression found in the texts recounting the exploits of some of the prophets, and those of Elijah in particular. Elijah, as we have seen was engaged in what might be described as 'soul flight' during the dreams of 1 Kings 19, and his inappropriate, ascending flight to the 'place' (Horeb?) where God is ultimately obliges the LORD to ask him (1 Kgs 19:9, 13) what he's doing there. The LORD is addressing a very revealing question to Elijah, the "man of God" and victor of Carmel, who in the depths of his despair appears to believe that God has deserted him, so much so that *he* has (unnecessarily) traveled to meet the God who was always ever present to him. If we now contrast Jonah's behavior with that of Elijah we are immediately presented with 'flight' in quite the opposite direction, since Jonah flees from God in a constant downwards direction. Jonah's 'flight' throughout chapters 1 and 2 of the book is, I believe, also 'soul flight' within a sequence of dreams, which ultimately culminate in his hypnopompic disgorgement from the fish in Jonah 2:11. Most people have experienced hypnopompia at one time or another—it is the partially awake, but still dreamy state usually experienced just as one wakes up in the morning, and within which the most bizarre features of the night's dreaming intrude into waking 'reality.' These two altered states of consciousness (dreaming and hypnopompia) are then followed by a third state—meditation, for in a manner similar to Elijah, Jonah commences a (gargantuan) feat of 'trance' running that takes him to Nineveh. When he arrives in that city, and at some point after the public proclamation of a fast, the prophet falls asleep and dreams a second time (Jonah 4:3–11), engaging once again in 'soul flight' out of the city. It is at this point (Jonah 4:3) that the differences between the experiences of Elijah and Jonah become most apparent.

In four separate dreams Elijah moves ever nearer to conversation with God. Firstly, he contends with Jezebel's *evil*, spiritual messenger, and then he has dealings with a second, (*neutral*) messenger, before finally taking instructions from the *good* messenger of the LORD. As these spiritual messengers or angels (the same Hebrew word is used throughout) change from evil through neutral to good they mark Elijah's progress towards an ever closer proximity to the LORD, with whom ultimately he converses. In Jonah's case, however, the situation is very different, for when Jonah prays (Jonah 4:2–3) the LORD is clearly immanent replying to him *immediately* in person. Jonah, of course, doesn't like that reply (Jonah 4:4) and flees, but conversation does eventually resume with the still immanent LORD getting the better of it. Elijah has had a bruising, confidence destroying spiritual encounter with a witch's messenger and ascends to God where he engages in restorative conversation. Jonah on the other hand flees from an uncooperative absence of conversation with God (Jonah 1:1), undergoes a life-changing, conversion experience at the point of death (Jonah 2:3–10), before finally entering into intimate—if somewhat heated—dialogue with God (Jonah 4:3–11). The reader comes to the book of "Jonah" in the middle of a dream and leaves it in the middle of a dream, but in between the quality of Jonah's relationship with God has changed from a refusal to communicate at all to one of verbose dialogue. The book of "Jonah" is therefore about the prophet making process, or rather the transition from a prophet (one who merely engages with the spirit world) to a man of God, one who has an immanent, intimate, and serving—though not necessarily always 'happy'—relationship with the LORD. Expressed differently, the book of "Jonah" would appear to be a model that details the stages in the internal life of any nascent 'prophet,' and it records the (psychological) suffering endured along the path to conversation with God. I am unsure whether this process requires of necessity that the would be servant of the LORD enters the "gates of death," but it certainly appears to help, and Chris's own experience of proximity to death (chapter 5) bears comparison with Jonah's fishy encounter.

Suffering and Enhanced Spirituality

I have always found the term 'spirituality' to be a rather slippery one capable of numerous definitions, and so when discussing 'enhanced spirituality' as it featured in Chris's story, I would prefer to talk about 'enhanced spiritual receptivity or heightened prophetic attributes.' Certainly, as far as suffering is concerned Chris had experienced perhaps a little more than her 'fair share,' having lost a young nephew aged six in a road accident, and also having lost her father at the relatively young age of fifty two. Those early prayer group sessions were soon to reveal that Chris had unresolved psychological problems of a rather more serious nature than unresolved grief, which as a couple we had never addressed. Those family deaths were never discussed to the extent that they should have been, as we thrust ourselves into our new business venture in the early eighties. If we had believed that the 'therapeutic nature of work' would cure all, then we were to be sadly mistaken. Modern studies have indicated that highly stressful life events—such as those experienced by Chris—are known to induce conditions of enhanced spirituality, and many researchers have reported that such crises are associated with measures of spiritual maturity. Indeed, the growth in spiritual maturity resulting from these episodes have often been misconstrued as indicating psychiatric illness. But instead of pointing to psychopathology these growth experiences are about spiritual changes going on within the person, and in agreement with James and Samuels may be seen to be "indicators of healthy post-trauma psychological adjustment." The Jonah story, exemplifies how God can both create and enhance the reality of prophetic dialogue out of the spiritual crisis Jonah endured, and subsequently utilize that dialogue to resolve Jonah's ongoing psychological difficulties. Aristotle, based on observations of the prophetic personnel of his own time, understood depression in a less than clinical way, that is, as a melancholic or "atrabilious temperament," and this may indeed be the very essence of the prophetic process both now and in antiquity, inasmuch as such a temperament heightens or enhances spiritual receptivity. Once these enhanced prophetic faculties have been brought to the fore they can then become a resource for God's people in the person of his prophet, although this depends to a very great extent on there being a willingness to recognize that resource.

13

Fasting—An Aid to Dialogue?

GIVEN THAT JESUS HIMSELF exhorted his followers to fast—albeit after his death (Matt. 9:15), it seems odd that fasting finds so few practitioners amongst modern Christians. If we discount (momentarily) the possibility that Jesus intended that his followers were to fast as a sign of mourning for his passing, then we are left with few alternative meanings. Moreover, it seems hardly likely that Jesus, the fulfiller of the law, would be endorsing yet another dry religious observance—just another sacrifice to add to all the others. But this is precisely the way in which the modern church seems to view Lent. The season of Lent, during which Christians are encouraged to exercise special 'self discipline,' appears to have been modeled on Jesus' forty day fast in the wilderness, but that 'self discipline' often has little resemblance to the LORD's post-Jordan experience. Lent for most Christians amounts to a half-hearted surrender of some excess or indulgence, rather than the spiritually significant activity it was intended to be. Did Jesus, therefore, intend his followers to fast as an act of asceticism in its own right—a form of strict discipline to suppress 'the desires of the body,' in order to concentrate on 'higher things?' If this were so, then the record would have shown Jesus himself fasting on many more occasions than is in fact the case. The truth is found to be quite the reverse, since Jesus is usually depicted within the gospels as an itinerant rabbi moving from place to place, and spending time *dining* with the most disreputable characters around! Could it be perhaps, that the significance of Jesus' strange exhortation in Matthew 9:15, simply lies in the presence and absence of God? Is fasting merely a way of making the soon to be absent Jesus present again to everyone? Moreover, it should not be lost on anyone that this comparison of the presence of God in the immanent Jesus and the presence of God in the fast, is in the *conversational* context of table fellowship. For Jesus' hearers mourning and fasting were undoubtedly culturally and religiously linked, but, it may be that Jesus intended to convey the idea of mourning precisely because mourning is a post-bereavement activity, and often involves severe depression. Was it therefore also Jesus' intention to draw out the fact—well known to his hearers—that both grieving and fasting can share a common core of depression through which God is accessible? A closer look at fasting from a medical viewpoint may enable us to answer this question.

Fasting as Semi-Starvation

By the time of Jesus the practice of fasting following a death had become a culturally defined way of expressing feelings of sorrow. But it is a matter of common observation and experience that the great distress of bereavement causes loss of appetite that can bring about abstinence from food. Thus, when Jesus referred to the cultural norm of fasting following bereavement, it would be implicit for both him and his hearers that this would (normally) overlie the reality of depressed mood, either brought about by, or leading to food abstinence. Because depression and appetite for food are so intimately linked within the hypothalamus area of the brain, either one can lead to the other, and the trigger for both can be the loss of a loved one. All that can be said is that there is an 'association' between fasting brought about by loss of appetite (true anorexia) and depression. Interestingly, some modern research (Ivan Eisler–1995) into parental loss by death or family breakup, revealed a statistical linkup between death in the family and the occurrence of an eating disorder. In the same way the ancients noted this association between the 'activities' of mourning (grieving) and fasting, whilst still reserving a religious significance for the latter. It may, therefore, be concluded that there is a circular relationship between depression, loss of appetite, and food abstinence, which may be initiated at any point by grief:

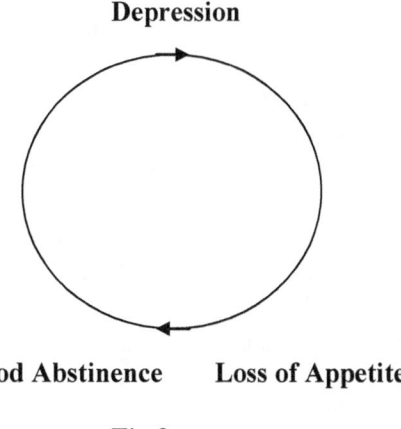

Fig.2

Fasting is normally considered to be a total abstinence from all food intake, but not including a normal intake of fluid (water). Such a situation may be medically understood to correspond to physiological starvation, which ultimately involves a progressive loss of body weight, and which may be observed—at least within modern Western societies—in those suffering from anorexia nervosa. But physiological starvation can ensue within a matter of hours, and can lead seamlessly into a state of depression. Indeed, sleep may be considered to be such a fast, one which often results in dreaming and which is terminated in the morning by *break*fast! As already noted, dreaming sleep is manifested by rapid eye movement (REM), which when enhanced; some have considered to be a 'biological marker' for depression. Fichter and Pirke have reported studies by other workers that relate an accelerated onset of REM sleep (and therefore dreaming) in patients undergoing reduced calorie intake (semi-starvation). Wax reports that this connection was not lost on the Rabbis, who in the Christian era, continued to value dreams as a means of revelation from God, but who were not impressed by the use of fasting as a method of inducing divine revelation through dreams, perceiving this to be 'forced.' In its everyday usage in the Ancient Near East religious fasting was known to be a controlled (and reversible) process. The aim of that process may have been an attempt to produce or enhance a particular psychophysiological condition, which we now medically understand and refer to as depression, as part and parcel of a more intense experience of dreaming.

Fasting in the Old Testament

When we look for examples of fasting in the Old Testament we find that there are numerous formal fast days, but that the word fast(ing) is rarely used in association with the luminaries of the prophetic tradition, such as Elijah, or Jonah. Even Moses appears to have gone without food only incidentally to the task(s) he was engaged in, that is, as a secondary result of a wilderness trek up Sinai to seek the LORD. In Elijah's case 'fasting' results from his involuntary participation in widespread famine (1 Kgs 18:2), whereas Jonah only fasts as a result of an unavoidable royal decree (Jonah 3:7), and Saul—the potential prophet/king—merely runs out of food during his long trek (1 Sam. 9:7). It would appear that the writers of all these texts have taken extreme care to separate and distance the involuntary 'fasting' from any later depression/dreaming—and its associated spiritual encounters.

The Elijah narratives (1 Kgs 17–19) are completely dominated by the theme of food or its absence, for although at first sight the story of the three year famine appears to be confined to chapter 17 the theme continues into the next chapter. All the different aspects of the absence of food are then dealt with in the first half of chapter 18. The return of life sustaining rain, the twice yearly rain of the eastern Mediterranean is the first point to be made, this is followed by the severity of the famine, and its consequences in terms of there being no fodder for domestic animals. We also read that Jezebel does not go hungry. As a Sidonian princess Jezebel has access to abundant food supplies from Tyre—the island grain *entrepôt* of the north eastern Mediterranean—and as a result is probably feeding king Ahab's entire court. Again we read that Obadiah, Ahab's lieutenant, is twice mentioned in connection with the feeding of the outlawed "prophets of the LORD." In the second half of chapter 18 it may be argued that the same theme of food runs continuously throughout the confrontation passage (18:23, 25–26, 29, 33, 36, 38), if only because the food (a bull) is 'consumed' by the "god who answers by fire." Finally, the chapter closes with Ahab's repast and the actual return of the life sustaining, food producing rain. Chapter 19 has the least number of food/famine references, but they are there in sufficient quantity (5 verses) for it to be clearly seen as a continuation of this dominant theme. When added together, all the verses about food (or the lack of it) must be deemed *the* dominant theme of 1 Kings 17–19, and they amount to fully 34% (31 Hebrew verses) of the subject matter of these three chapters.

The continuation of the starvation theme into Elijah's dreams in chapter 19, although it appears to be related to the depressed dreaming, seems to occupy a secondary role within the chapter. It is only in the middle of the night's dreaming that Elijah dreams about food, and his two longest dreams are dominated by depression, the first one (19:2b-4) by its 'diagnosis' or characterisation of depression, and the second (19:9c-21) by what amounts to the 'treatment' of that depression. Depressed people need to be drawn back into dialogue and other activities, and it is this objective that occupies the latter two thirds of chapter 19 as the LORD is seen to engage Elijah with an 'open' question. "What are you doing here, Elijah"? (19:9) is such an open question, which leaves Elijah with the opportunity to respond in his own way. Open questions are to be preferred over 'closed' questions, which in Gilbert's words do not allow a respondent to "articulate their own meanings," and he adds that in terms of counselling skill the employment of open questions comprises the "real bedrock of counselling." Clearly, the sheer weight of references to food, famine or starvation must reflect the deliberate intention on the part of the writer to affirm the existence of some kind of relationship between 'fasting,' depression, and spiritual encounter. But any such linkage is shown only as an exacerbating and subordinate factor in the run up to spiritual encounter.

In the last chapter Saul was shown to be another, depressed, (potential) prophet who first comes to the reader's attention in circumstances where both he and his companion had gone hungry for three days. 1 Samuel 9 shows the two of them on a wilderness trek during which they run out of food, before we see Saul portraying the excessive and inappropriate humility (9:21) so indicative of depression. I have argued in my own research that Saul's depression here leads seamlessly into the altered states of consciousness (9:22-26) of meditation and dreaming, but that the writer uses the next chapter (10) to show that Saul's mental state is not dependent on semi-starvation. Any idea that Saul's depression in chapter 9 results directly from his fasted condition is dispelled in the next chapter when we are told Saul meets three men who re-provision him. It is interesting that the young, fit, and sober Saul (he does not accept any wine!) eats only high carbohydrate food (he does not accept any meat!), which is known to have a mood-lifting effect. Saul is, therefore, as ascetically unprepared for altered state, spiritual encounter as anyone could be, by the time he meets and joins in with the group of prophets in 1 Sam. 10:10-13. As with Elijah then, these passages appear to show that depression and its associated dreamy/meditative states are related to, but not wholly or directly dependent on (enforced) 'fasting.' Depression and its association with dreamy or meditative states appears to be where the emphasis is placed, whilst at the same time there seems to be an acknowledgement that 'fasting' can provide a conducive environment for the attainment of altered state experiences.

In the light of my own research interest in this area I have often asked people how fasting has affected them personally, and the answers I received varied significantly. One particular respondent said she never felt better, experiencing a kind of euphoric clarity of thought, together with purged, cleansed, and 'healthier' bodily functions. But there was no depression. Another respondent, an advocate of alternative medicine, told me how within 48 hours of fasting, her mood had sunk to dangerously low levels, so much so, that she was compelled to discontinue the exercise after only five days. But in this case there was no altered state of consciousness, or enhanced dreaming. A third person on fasting soon found himself in a whole new world of 'delusions,' and he too was compelled to give it up. It would seem that the evidence, both ancient and modern, is suggesting that fasting tends to exacerbate depression in those who are perhaps already (genetically?) predisposed to it, and it may also be the case that this is true of quite a small number of people.

'Fasting' and the New Testament

In chapter 12 I advanced the argument that to be prone to depression is to be prone to characteristically altered REM (dreaming) sleep, and explained how my own research has demonstrated that numbers of the prophets of the Old Testament (including Elijah) were depressive dreamers. The suggestion was also made that this prophetic trait or condition (depression/dreaming) was related to meaningful, altered-state, spiritual encounter with the Deity by the employment of meditative practices or states. When this modern understanding of the relationship between dreams and prophecy is allied to the apparent scriptural equivalence of the 'prophet' and 'dreamer of dreams' we can place new interpretations on other Old Testament stories. One such story is that of Joseph and his brothers. It is certain that Joseph is nowhere described as a prophet, yet the emphasis of the Hebrew term 'dreamer' (Gen. 37:19) scornfully uttered by Joseph's brothers, lies in its prophetic connotations. Hamilton translates it as "master of dreams," and notes with approval Von Rad's understanding of the term as "one empowered to prophetic dreams"—a meaning which is far more evocative than that denoted by the English word 'dreamer.' Thus, these scholars are heard to say from the Hebrew that Joseph is a prophet, in that he both dreams, and (later) interprets dreams. Of course, these views would be considerably strengthened if, in the light of our argument about depression/dreaming, Joseph can be shown to have been depressed. In order to do this it will be necessary to look at some of the psychological and sociological factors found in the Joseph stories.

An environmental view of mood disorders offers four major theories which seek to account for abnormal behavior, these are psychoanalytical theory, cognitive theory, behaviorist theory, and family structure theory respectively. On turning to Genesis, we discover an abundance of material in the Joseph stories, which confirm that the patriarch Joseph suffered maternal loss (Gen. 35:18), a key precursor of depression according to the psychoanalytical theory. This neo-Freudian emphasis on an interpersonal origin of mental disorder is held by Gallagher to support the view that an upheaval in the parent/child relationship can damage the "developing personality and cause lifelong mental anguish." Moreover, maternal loss for Joseph would involve 'the loss of accustomed positive social reinforcements' in an alien environment, where the remaining three wives of Jacob were competing for preference for both themselves and their children—to the exclusion of Joseph and Benjamin. In this behaviorist view, the loss of his mother would result for Joseph, in a severe realignment of the domestic (kitchen!) hierarchy, as the other siblings petitioned their mothers for advantage. Depression need not be preceded by the loss of a loved one, but such a loss is one route through which in Gallagher's opinion a person's "positive social reinforcements may be eliminated." Thirdly, the family structure theory points to an increased incidence of depression in especially favored members of families, such as Joseph (Gen. 37:3), whose mother was also his father's favorite. This theory helps to explain why only one of the children in the families of depressives typically develops depression. Such a child, occupying a special position amongst the other children, would inevitably experience the hostility and envy (Gen. 37:4) of his siblings. Finally, birth order and sibship size have also been identified as significant factors in the development of depression in the younger members of large families. Indeed, for Gallagher "it appears that the first born in a small family and the last born in a large family are particularly vulnerable to mental disorder." On the assumption that the Jacob/Rachel axis can be identified as a discrete unit within the polygamous whole, Joseph seems to qualify on both counts, since he was Rachel's first born whilst still being the eleventh of Jacob's twelve sons. Thus, Joseph's susceptibility to mental 'illness' can be demonstrated to have been extremely high on the basis of both birth order studies, and three of the four major environmental theories of the causation of mood disorders. An early history of depression following maternal loss would also predispose Joseph to a recurrence or relapse, when presented with a similarly traumatic episode such as that recorded in Genesis 37:20-28. This further and final deprivation of home and family following his sale into slavery in Egypt would probably ensure Joseph's continuing intimacy with severe and life long depression. Although a case has been made for viewing Joseph as a depressive dreamer (prophet), 'fasting' understood as physiological starvation would seem on the face of it not to figure in the Joseph stories, yet there is one tenuous link between Joseph's depression and such fasting, and strangely, that link occurs in Acts 7:9–12.

Most modern English translations of the Hebrew term used in Genesis 42:21 show Joseph experiencing 'anguish' (NRSV) or 'distress' (NIV) at the hands of his brothers. A fuller translation of both the Hebrew and Greek gives the more enlightening phrase, 'anguish of soul' (as per the KJV), thus, making clear the internal, psychological nature of Joseph's condition. Luke, in his treatment of the Joseph stories in Acts 7 uses the Greek word *thlipsis* to describe this internal anguish. In common with the other New Testament writers, Luke was thoroughly familiar with the Greek 'Old Testament'—the Septuagint, but adds new information when he uses this word to refer to Joseph's *plural* experience of affliction*s* (Acts 7:10). It seems apparent from the text (v.10) that Joseph suffered from ongoing anxieties and depressions consistent with the record of enforced separations from firstly his birth family (Gen. 37), and secondly his later, adopted family (Gen. 39). In the very next verse Luke uses exactly the same word (*thlipsis*) to describe the effects of the famine, which afflicted Canaan in Joseph's time. Luke appears, therefore, to have classified Joseph's psychological condition as being of the same general, nature as that later suffered by his brothers (Gen. 42:21, Acts 7:11), and additionally indicated that the brothers' condition may have derived, at least in part, from the famine. Luke (the physician?) seems to have classified Joseph's *thlipsis*—that is, his ongoing anxiety/anguish/depression—with the depression that may result from physiological starvation such as that experienced by his brothers during the famine. Again, it must be emphasized that it seems hardly likely that the same word used in adjacent verses would have different meanings. Reduced calorie intake, by famine (i.e. involuntary fasting) would seem to be linked with depression, however tenuously, in the mind of at least one New Testament writer! Semi-starvation or involuntary fasting continues to be related to depression in the New Testament, but as with the Old Testament it again fails to be definitively labelled as a precursor of prophetic, spiritual encounter. Although fasting continues to be associated with the prayers of prophets (Acts 13:1–3) it may, as in the Old Testament, be simply exacerbating the prophetic traits of those already predisposed to depression and meaningful, spiritual encounter. As such, fasting via an exacerbating effect on pre-existing depression may serve as an aid to dialogue with the Deity for some people, but probably only a very small group of people.

14

Composite Prophecy

DURING THE EARLY YEARS of the New Testament church, the designation *prophetes* was given to individual Christians within the then prevalent Old Testament understanding of the prophet's role, and the essence of prophetic activity remained that which it had always been. Indeed, because the New Testament does not differentiate in either vocabulary or phraseology between references to Old and New Testament prophecy or prophets, it has to be conceded that the prophet's role remained unchanged. I have so far maintained that the role of the Old Testament prophet was dialogical—a function of relationship to God—and that this function was facilitated by what we now call depression. Fasting, whether voluntary or involuntary was found to enhance the depression of those already predisposed to it. Since the New Testament fails to differentiate in its terminology between past and present prophets, it follows that the Christian prophets found in the accounts of the early church functioned in precisely the same way, that is, in a dialogical manner, as a result of the very same psychophysiological disposition. Luke in particular, saw the relationship between prophecy and fasting, where he records fasting and praying as the natural activity of the prophetess Anna (Luke 2:36–37). It is clear that the prophetess Anna, as a woman, would be confined to the outer courts of the Jerusalem temple precincts, which she never left, and where she was always to be found fasting and praying. Yet this woman was party to new divinely revealed information about the child, Jesus (Luke 2:38), in particular his role as liberator of the people of God, precisely because of her prophetic activities of fasting and prayer. The clear implication of the Lukan record is that Anna divulged this information to Joseph and Mary from within, and because of, her fasted condition. Indeed, the Greek speaks of Anna coming up to them at the hour, or very time of her fasting.

It is interesting that when Luke speaks of fasting and prayer, it is always in that order (Luke 2:37; 5:33, Acts 13:3), except where we find "the ones having prayed" (Gk. *proseuxamenoi*) doing so "with fastings," in Acts 14:23. The clear intention is for fasting to create the right 'environment' for a divine communication, whether in the form of a vision, dream or word, about which the prophet may then pray. This is made explicit by Luke in Acts 13:1–3 where we see that:

> In the church at Antioch there were prophets... (Acts 13:1)
> While they were... fasting, the Holy Spirit said,... (Acts 13:2)
> Then after... praying... (Acts 13:3)

Thus, a revelation/feedback/revelation sequence (a dialogue!) is set up, which permits a great deal of precision to be employed in the prayers. In short, God gave them their prayer topic, about which they then prayed, releasing God's enormous power on the project in hand. The three verses of Acts 13:1–3 are a mini study in mutuality, that is, in cooperation with God for His immediate purposes of that moment.

Matthew, perhaps the most 'Jewish' of the gospel writers, approaches the subject of prophecy using a different tack. As already noted, Matthew records Jesus himself exhorting his followers to fast—albeit after his death—yet significantly in a dialogical or conversational context. More important, however, are the numerous occasions when Matthew makes reference to dreams and dreaming, especially during the birth narratives (Matt. 1:20; 2:12, 13, 19, 22) where both Joseph and the three 'wise men' are divinely instructed. Matthew is using dreams—a 'tool' or means of prophesying—to demonstrate the fulfilment of messianic prophecy, and he uses that same 'tool' to likewise proclaim Jesus innocent before Pilate (Matt. 27:19). Clearly, both Matthew and Luke are placing emphasis upon the links between fasting, dreaming, and prophecy, very early in their gospel accounts. Luke demonstrates the importance of the correlation between prophecy and dreaming for the infant church when he reports Peter's revised restatement of Joel 2:28 in Acts 2:17:

> In the last days it will be, God declares, that I will pour out my
> Spirit upon all flesh, and your sons and your daughters shall

prophesy, and your young men shall see visions, and your old men shall dream dreams. (Acts 2:17 NRSV)

Peter's emphasis lies on the 'all flesh' nature of the new covenant, explaining that all the descendants (sons and daughters) of the people of God (the church) would from this point forward prophesy. The whole church could and would prophesy, especially the church elders (Gk. *presbuteroi* or presbyters)—who need not necessarily have been old men, through (fasting facilitated?) dreams! This verse needs to be seen as being 'vertically stacked,' that is, each phrase should be understood as being superimposed upon the previous phrase, and where the Spirit will become the agent of prophecy (dialogue), which is then worked out in visions and dreams. Put another way, God is saying that when you seek me inside your fasts, I will become present to you and speak with you! But if the New Testament church understood their own prophets as being in direct succession to, and identical with the Old Testament prophets, how had the Pentecost Event changed things? In what ways did the dialogue that is prophecy change after Pentecost?

Practical Prophecy—New Testament Style!

One of the main problems with Christianity—at least for non-Christians—is its apparent blurring and fudging of monotheism, since before Jesus there was only the Jewish God, who despite having a personal name (implying others existed), was considered to be the sole arbiter of human affairs. Then the Christ came into this world and was acknowledged not simply as another god, but rather a second person that shared the attribute of divinity. Jesus vowed He would send a third person of the Godhead to counsel mankind in his absence, and this third person, the Holy Spirit, has remained to communicate with men ever since. But God's self-giving of himself in the person of the Holy Spirit as outlined in Peter's speech at Pentecost (Acts 2:17) is only for believers, that is, for those people who desire relationship with him. Peter's speech at Pentecost was directed to people who desired relationship with God, and who had traveled the length and breadth of the Mediterranean world (often taking a year out to do so!) to seek it. The then current system of achieving relationship with God—the temple based sacrificial system—was exclusive and corrupt, and therefore a kind of 'democratisation' of the presence of God was needed. I deliberately place 'democratisation' in quotation marks, because democracy in common with many other Greek ideas has no place whatsoever in Christianity, since Jesus came into the world as a Regent (Messiah), and continues to rule as a co-regnal and absolute Monarch. Thus, although a poor analogy, the revolutionary idea of 'democratising' his presence to the people of Israel, conveys the essence of God's intention to "pour out (his) Spirit upon all flesh," and not just some (chief priestly) flesh!

The Holy Spirit then is only for believers, and it is interesting to note that Paul similarly considers that "prophecy is not for unbelievers but for believers" (1 Cor. 14:22), having the capacity to establish, confirm, and edify believers in their faith, or more accurately their trust in God. Moreover, Paul has other things to say about prophecy, and considers that the church itself is built upon apostles and prophets (Eph. 2:20), in that order. In his first letter to the Corinthians, Paul exhorts them to "strive for the spiritual gifts, and especially that you may prophesy" (1 Cor. 14:1), so highly does he value prophecy. The letter to the Romans demonstrates through the use of the first person plural, that Paul expects the whole church to be able to prophesy, although to differing degrees, that is, "in proportion to faith" (Rom. 12:6 KJV). What emerges from the Pauline letters is a prophecy-centred church in which all the participants prophesy, but the only thing which sets the designated prophet apart is not so much the 'office' of prophet, as a gifting developed over the course of much time spent with God. It is this, which enables Paul to denote prophets as 'foundations' of the church, along with apostles, and is almost certainly a reference to an eldership, which has nothing to do with age.

It has been my contention thus far that the quintessential feature of the Old Testament prophets was their psychophysiologically sustained dialogues with the LORD, and that this continued to be the practice of the New Testament prophets (Acts 13:1–3). But what does this mean for the practicalities of conducting prophecy, in a situation where according to Paul *everyone* should participate? Can scripture provide us with an example of such a session of practical prophecy? I believe that Paul has left us a metaphorical record of how such a session should be conducted, in four brief verses at the end of his first letter to the Thessalonians. These four verses are found in 1 Thessalonians 5:19–22 and comprise five directives:

> 19 Do not quench the Spirit.
> 20 Do not despise the words of prophets,
> 21 but test everything; hold fast to what is good;
> 22 abstain from every form of evil.

Both Morris, and later Wanamaker have suggested that these directives are linked, and that the theme of the first of these two imperatives is continued in the latter three, and this is consistent with Best's view that taken together the five imperatives form a complete whole. Superficially then, an examination of the structure of the Greek text reveals that the five imperatives of vv.

19–22 form a single, unified metaphor, and further support for this can be found in the Greek terms used throughout all four verses. Before examining these terms it may be noted with Penney that this single and unified metaphor describes a testing of the prophecies *not* the prophets.

In the New Testament the use of the Greek verb, *sbennumi*, (to quench) is rare in a literal sense and restricted to this one verse (1 Thess 5:19) in a metaphorical sense, and as a consequence comparisons in a Christian setting are simply not found. In common usage, however, the root sense of the verb in its Graeco-Roman setting gives the meaning, to extinguish by drowning in water. Interestingly, 'quenching' is a metallurgical term in long usage from antiquity, and describes the plunging of red or white hot metal into water by the blacksmith, in order to effect the fastest possible cooling of the metal. One of the purposes of quenching is to cool quickly and dispose of a piece of iron which *cannot be worked further*, and Paul's instruction not to despise prophecy (v. 20) would thus be alluding to the rejection with contempt (Greek, *exoutheneo*) of the metal object in the underlying analogy. The action depicted here compares the prophecy to the now worthless metal object, which is being quenched and thrown into the scrap box at the back of the shop, by an exasperated blacksmith! It is at this point that Paul enjoins his Thessalonian friends not to give up, but to continue to work the prophecy by 'testing' or 'proving' (Greek, *dokimazo*) the metal artefact in v. 21.

Once again in *dokimazo* the twin themes of metal and fire appear, since in its Old Testament (Septuagintal) usage it represents the Hebrew *bahan,* meaning to test for genuineness by fire, and in its classical, Greek setting was used in connection with the testing of metals or metal coinage. It has been suggested by some commentators that the testing process of v. 21 is analogous to the testing of metal coinage, and parallels have been drawn between verses 21–22 and a reported (but unwritten) saying of Jesus: "Be approved money changers." This agraphon, which had wide circulation in the early church, was according to Best "used in the sense of rejecting the spurious and retaining the good." Unfortunately, the parallel would seem to fall down, since verse 21 does not contain the essential word 'money changers.' The connection, however, could be an idiomatic and shared understanding—in the minds of both Paul and his Thessalonian friends—of *the kind of testing* being conducted here. Because the Roman emperors were no strangers to fiscal problems, they often indulged in the adulteration of the coinage to reduce the use of bullion, and a common qualitative 'test' for precious metal content, then, as until comparatively recently, was to listen to the *sound* of the coin when dropped—to see if it 'rang true'.

The same type of sounding 'test' is thought by Cleere to have been carried out by ancient blacksmiths in the production of tools and swords during (or more likely comprising) the hammering of the previously unworked metal. Iron making in ancient times was not a fusion process as it is today, indeed, furnaces were usually Heath Robinson affairs often built into hillsides and used only once. They produced a single lump of metal weighing about 20 kg. called a bloom, and this 'solid' metal was a spongy mass containing slag inclusions (impurities), which had been incompletely removed by the initial smelt. The block was then separated into smaller portions by cold chiselling to form 'worked' blooms. These 'worked' blooms weighing about 1 kg. were the typical raw material of the smith, but still contained unknown and variable amounts of slag inclusions, distributed very unevenly throughout the metal. In the blacksmith's hands the small bloom of iron would be heated up in the forge to about 1150° C (yellowish white in color), and then hammered into shape, simultaneously expressing any residual, semi molten slag inclusions from the solid, yet malleable iron. Microscopic Examination of metals with high concentrations of non-metallic inclusions (slags) has shown that small cracks form readily when inclusions are present. Moreover, not only do inclusions nucleate or initiate cracks, but also they aid in their growth and elongation, for the cracks readily jump from one inclusion to the next. This illustrates why the smith might disregard or reject a partially worked bloom if it was full of slag inclusions and he thought it might breakup completely, becoming unworkable. As the slag was expressed the hammer tone would probably change from a dull thud to a more metallic ring, and the pitch or frequency of that ring would increase in proportion to the amount of alloyed carbon in the metal. The smith would therefore be testing the progress of his work by the *sound* of the hammer blows, and two things are occurring during this test. Firstly, hot semi molten slag inclusions are being expressed (flying in all directions!) from the hot, yellow (1100° C) solid, yet malleable and plastic bloom on the anvil. Secondly, from the sight, feel, and especially sound of the hammering process, an experienced smith would have been able to ascertain (test or prove) the bloom's usefulness for making a cutting edge implement, for example a sword. If the bloom failed this 'proving,' the smith had two choices, he could either quench the metal and reject it, or he could engage in the slow, careful process of individually carburising this particular piece of metal in his forge, in order to case harden or 'steel' it—a relatively long and painstaking process.

Thus, one aspect of the underlying, idiomatic, and elegant connected themes of the testing of coins, iron/steel on the anvil, and indeed prophecies is the qualitative *sound* of them. In the case of iron, that sound may indicate the need for further work to produce cutting edge quality steel. The ancient blacksmith's art consisted largely of the cementation or carburisation of wrought iron, which was achieved by continually reinserting the wrought iron into the carbon-rich heart of the forge. By repeated working/reinsertion in this manner, the smith would produce a laminated mixture of iron and steel with the required properties of toughness and hardness. The object of the whole exercise was to remove the slag (bad!), whilst introducing the steel making carbon (good!). In the case of prophecy, it is the 'word' that is crafted by continual enquiry of, or reinsertion into, what is in effect the 'Forge of God,' which is of course blown through by the 'Breath of God' or Holy Spirit. Thus, Paul exhorts the Thessalonians to keep working on the composite 'word' until eventually it has become perfectly crafted for its purpose.

In this metaphorical context of the smith working at the anvil, it is possible to make better sense of the last two Pauline directives in verses 21b and 22. The verb most frequently translated as 'hold fast' in verse 21b (Greek, *katecho*) becomes clearer when its other nuances of 'grasp,' 'restrain,' 'hold down,' and 'control' are applied to a scene where a hot metal object must be held securely in long-handled tongs. It is the 'good' metal object that is being held firmly here—understood in the sense of what is sound and beneficial—while the slag impurities are hammered away. The verb often translated as 'abstain' in verse 22 (Gk.—*apecho*), but which fundamentally means 'keep away from,' sits in stark opposition to the 'hold fast' of verse 21b, and is reinforced by the preposition *apo* (Gk.—away from) which actively emphasizes movement. Thus, the blacksmith can be pictured in the forge scene as holding fast or grasping the (good) work with the left hand, as he holds himself away from the hot, flying slag (bad), as each hammer blow is struck with the right. Interestingly, the 'bad' of verse 22 (Greek, *poneros*), which is often translated as evil, is, in classical Hellenistic usage derived from work or toil, and as such, is capable of accurately depicting the toilsome, grievous, and painful labor of the forge scene. Both classical Greek and Old Testament (Septuagintal) usage also affirm a sense of the 'dangerous' in this word.

Paul's complex metaphor is, I believe, building on his more famous metaphor—that of the 'body of many parts' (1 Cor. 12:12–28), but is here showing the body in *action*. The body, or corporate church is compared here to the blacksmith, whose whole body is in action, as he employs his arms, legs, torso (swerving to avoid the flying fragments of slag), mind, eyes, and especially ears to the job of perfecting the work. In like manner, the body of the church is expected to work together as a coordinated whole to produce a perfectly crafted 'word' of prophecy through question and answer dialogue. Interestingly, Paul confirms he is thinking along these lines in the very next verse (1 Thess. 5:23) immediately following his 'blacksmith' metaphor, where he addresses the whole corporate church.

> And the very God of peace sanctify you wholly; and I pray God your whole spirit and soul and body be preserved blameless unto the coming of our Lord Jesus Christ. (1 Thess. 5:23 KJV)

Some scholars have seen parallels here with another of Paul's metaphors for the church, that is, the 'living temple' analogy of 2 Corinthians 6:16, in which Paul draws together a number of Old Testament scriptures describing God's dwelling amongst his people. The essence of that dwelling as depicted in 1 Thessalonians 5:23 is that it should be "complete and in every part." Although Paul doesn't elaborate on structural technicalities, it is clear that the intention is to convey the idea of 'bonding' (both within and between the stones), and through which each individual stone is held firmly in place to form a unified whole. The purpose of the unified, corporate 'living temple' is quite simply to 'contain God'—both within and between the saints—thus reinforcing Paul's frequent and emphatic insistence that prophecy is for all!

The Discrediting of New Testament Prophecy

I have suggested in the foregoing blacksmithing analogy that the conduct of prophecy in the Pauline churches involved the whole body. Indeed, the whole church was engaged in a corrective process, working dialogically with the Spirit of God to progressively remove error from the 'word' as originally perceived, and to imbue it with further divine insights. This process is probably being depicted in Paul's letter to the Corinthians, containing the passage commencing at 1 Corinthians 14:29, where a most revealing insight into the orderly conduct of prophecy is to be found. Interestingly, it seems to be the recognized prophets who speak first (v 29), but their utterances are then subject to an evaluation, or more likely, a (spiritual) discernment (Greek, *diakrino*) by *all* the others in the body. The object of the exercise is to separate that which is of God from that which is not (i.e. human in origin), and then to infuse this with a further revelation from 'another person sitting nearby.' By implication it would seem that the 'person sitting nearby' may not be one of the recognized prophets, and this is supported in the following verse (v. 31), where Paul emphasizes that *all* may prophesy. The whole situation is corporate, social, and above all takes place in the Spirit, and the Spirit working through all the 'ordinary' members of the body is able to correct and eradicate any error produced by the 'few,' whilst at the same time 'beefing up' the original composite word.

Prophecy, as envisaged by Paul here in 1 Corinthians and in 1 Thessalonians 5:19–22 simply does not take place in the modern Christian scene, and there are a number of reasons for this. Firstly, there is the Thessalonian problem itself where the members of that church simply despaired of ever engaging in meaningful prophecy, and were constantly and prematurely rejecting the initial words from God. In such a situation it is easy to envisage circumstances where the practice of prophecy by the whole church would be discontinued, leaving the church 'flying blind' as it were. Elsewhere (Rom. 12:6) Paul exhorts the saints to "prophesy, in proportion to faith"; or basically to prophesy in a confident manner—confident that is, that they were speaking the Spirit's words. If a situation arose where that confidence was undermined, many would withdraw completely from prophetic activity, leaving the 'professionals' (the more recognized prophets) not subject to sanction by the whole body. Ultimately, that path will lead to error, and there are many instances where churches guided by a few such prophets have been led astray—for example the church movement led by Montanus and his two associates in the late second century AD. The Montanist movement, which started in Phrygia, was probably a blend of rural Christian prophecy with the local, pagan variety, which had long been a feature of this region of Asia Minor. Montanus had announced the imminent (and local) return of Christ, and was condemned and discredited by other churchmen in the wider church hierarchy when this didn't take place. In such circumstances, where prophecy does become discredited, it can be an all too easy option to dispense with it altogether. It would certainly seem as if prophecy is, at one and the same time, the church's greatest strength and its greatest weakness, and the only safeguard against its abuse would appear to be whole church participation—"in proportion to faith"!

Nevertheless, if in the Pauline purview, prophecy is an activity in which *all* the 'body' are to engage, it must be asked whether it is realistically possible to achieve this in modern churches numbering hundreds, if not thousands of people? Well, in answer to this question, I can only draw on my own, rather limited experience, which points to a solution based on small, home prayer groups. Now it might be objected that great emphasis is already placed on small home groups in many modern churches, and I would be the first to acknowledge that such groups have without doubt revitalized the Christian scene. The problem with many such groups, however, is the way in which they are formed and propagated. Formation of such groups is as often as not around 'established and knowledgeable' leaders from within the larger congregation, to whom new group members are either allocated (by the church leaders) or co-opted (by the group leaders). Thus, a kind of 'slightly forced,' 'clubby,' social environment is formed, in which only very 'safe' activities such as praising, group bible study, and (often very general) prayer take place. In order to facilitate the formation of audacious, risk-taking, Christian home groups, I think a much more 'bottom up' approach to home group formation is needed. Such an approach to home group construction would involve a much more careful assessment of the dynamics of the church membership, placing emphasis on the identification of pre-existing friendships. Frequently described as 'chemistry', the formation of a friendship is a strange and essentially spiritual thing, which can often take place in about 9.3 seconds—in other words it just happens! Building a home group on such a basis would therefore be taking advantage of existing human spiritual bondings or relationships. Luke gives a brief insight into this when he describes the post Pentecost scene in Acts 2:41–42:

> . . . and that day about three thousand persons were added. (42) They devoted themselves to the apostles' teaching and fellowship, to the breaking of bread and the prayers.

Now clearly fellowship (the Greek word *koinonia* means the forming of a close mutual relationship) and especially table fellowship, cannot take place in groups numbering three thousand! Obviously, some form of multiple, unstructured, and almost spontaneous group formation must have occurred, even though they will have continued to meet together (perhaps in the temple courts) in a larger assembly. In other words I am suggesting that now, as then, we should allow our home fellowship groups to choose each other, aided perhaps, but not directed, by the lightest, most astute perceptions of the church leaders. Once formed the emphasis must remain on fellowship, especially table fellowship, to strengthen and develop the existing spiritual relationship and to cement new members into the existing matrix of relationships. It is the formation of these deep mutual bonds that is the essential prerequisite for the Holy Spirit's activities in the 'body.'

15

Intimacy with God

THE ENGLISH WORD 'FELLOWSHIP' has become a rather weak and under used term, which, where understood at all, often denotes something between loose affability and camaraderie of the 'boys night out' kind. A fuller expansion of the New Testament understanding of the word 'fellowship' (Greek, *koinonia*) would, however, convey a much greater sense of a very close mutual relationship. Further scriptural nuances of the word such as 'participation,' 'sharing in,' 'contribution,' or 'gift' give some sense of the depth of these strong relationships. The essential meaning of the Greek word is in some respects nowadays better conveyed by the word 'economy,' which is actually derived from it, and which better depicts the sense of *interdependency* intended. Fundamental to daily life in New Testament times was the household economy and central to that economy was the interdependency of the husband/wife relationship of marriage. It would not be an exaggeration to say that to be in fellowship is to be in multiple 'partnership' with others, each relationship being in no small measure an approximation of the marriage partnership, and it therefore comes as no surprise to find that 'partnership' is yet another meaning of *koinonia*. Such partnerships by virtue of the sheer amount of time spent in each others company engender a (spiritual) intimacy, which can be utilized in Christian, home, fellowship groups to achieve a similar degree of intimacy with God. Herein lies Luke's emphasis in Acts 2:42, which may be paraphrased: "They devoted themselves to the apostles' teaching and to fellowship, to table fellowship and to prayers."

Now Jesus was a pretty astute sort of guy, and when He put together his original group of disciples, He used this same principle. Luke's gospel records (Luke 5:10) how James, John and Simon (Peter) were already partners (Greek, *koinonoi*) in the same economy (Greek, *koinonia*), that is, in the fishing business! Moreover, James and John were brothers, as also were Peter and Andrew (Matt. 4:18), revealing even more intimate familial relationships within the same household economies. The problem is that such close, strong relationships are rarely found in modern society, or indeed the modern church, which sadly, too often reflects it. As a society we have been involved in a long process, which over the past two thousand years has eradicated tribes, clans (communities?), and extended families, until finally the basic ('nuclear') family itself is under attack. All this has taken place against a background in which national identity has become preeminent, leading to a situation where the modern state reigns supreme over individuals, the former being immensely powerful and the latter very weak. Against such a background in society as a whole, is it possible for the Christian church to stand out as wholly different, by virtue of its possession of strong, multiple, and lasting bonds of relationship? In order to achieve this, however, there is no substitute for time spent together in each others company—as in post Pentecost Jerusalem—but all too often this simply does not happen.

Pentecost was of course a weeklong, Jewish festival that celebrated both the barley harvest and the beginning of the wheat harvest, and it was attended by diaspora Jews from all over the Roman world and beyond. The essence of these Jewish festivals and indeed the more personal events such as Jewish marriages, was that they were weeklong events of carefully and painstakingly organized feasting. Thus, what Luke records in Acts 2:41–42 is the extended fellowshipping together of groups of the three thousand converts in each others lodgings, and the consequent building of strong relationships through the sheer amount of *time* spent in table fellowship. Moreover, if Jesus deliberately chose some strong existing relationships built upon much time spent together, and then went on to spend even more time in table fellowship with his disciples (Luke 5:33), it seems that we should draw the obvious conclusions when constructing our own home groups. Home groups can it seems, benefit from the inclusion of existing relationships from the start, that is, by including where possible brothers, sisters, established married couples, and even business partners. But to make progress toward the making of a single, spiritually connected 'body' on the Pauline model, requires significantly more time spent in each others company, whether that is in joint activities or simple table fellowship.

So, where is all this leading? Why is time spent in each other's company so important? What is the difference between 'giving up' say four hours a week for church (the Sunday morning service plus the weekly home group meeting), compared for example, with dining together on a regular basis or having regular meetings in the pub? The answer to these questions is the achievement of an easy relationship with each other involving closeness and intimacy, which themselves engender openness and honesty. Where such an atmosphere exists, it becomes possible to relax and think "I can't (and don't want to) hide anything from him, he knows me too well"! or "I'm not embarrassed or shy in this company, because I both know and am known by my friends, therefore I can be confident, yes even bold"! Now confidence has already been noted in connection with prophecy (Rom. 12:6), but boldness (Greek, *parresia*) is spoken of by many New Testament writers (Acts 4:31, Heb. 4:16, 1 John 5:14) in addition to Paul (2 Cor. 3:12; Eph. 3:12; Phil. 1:20), and carries the additional meanings of openness and frankness. In short, home fellowship groups must be confident, bold, open, free, and frank with each other, before they can be so with God—hence the order of Luke's sequence in Acts 2:42! It may have been these very visible, strong bonds of relationship that led to one of the first groups of Jesus' followers being labelled as Christians (Latin, *Christiani*) at Antioch (Acts 11:26). Is it possible that to be identified in this way bears the quintessential Christian witness? Perhaps Christians should display their fellowship in or at all the public interfaces of society, every place in fact, where people meet together, precisely to avoid being seen as a private 'holy huddle' where the sole emphasis is on a somewhat esoteric discipleship. In this way, and as a means of countering the culture of pluralism in our society, Christians who prominently display their fellowship publicly would be the true heirs of the original people of God, engendering desire in those (millions) who search desperately for spiritual fulfilment in our times.

It is therefore, my contention that the very essence of primitive Christianity is tightly encapsulated in Luke's description (Acts 2:41–42) of the post-Pentecost scene, and that there is no reason why this prescription should not continue to apply to modern believers. That prescription began with 'seekers' who, desiring God, embarked upon a pilgrimage to the 'abode of God'—originally seen to be the Jerusalem temple. Having reached their destination, they accept the personal and internal witness of the Holy Spirit that Jesus is LORD and Messiah, demonstrate this publicly through baptism, and proceed to have the scriptures (the Old Testament) reinterpreted to them through the Christ event. It is only after fellowship groups of these like minded persons have come together in the most intimate of circumstances (table fellowship), that corporate prayer to God can take place. The essence of the whole process being the formation of a unified corporate group, or 'body of believers,' prior to approaching God together in prayer. It is easy to see how this can be a repeatable and self-propagating process, and that the original bond of the twelve disciples, the post-Pentecost groupings (which almost certainly led to the formation of the Roman church), and even Paul's own shared missions displayed and exemplified fellowship first and foremost. God himself lives inside these (spiritual) fellowships (Paul's 'living temple') in the post-Pentecost environment, and it is this to which the Holy Spirit wishes to witness still in the modern world, thus making the public display of our bonding absolutely essential.

Fellowship and Prophecy

If Luke has made explicit the link between prophecy—understood as dialogue with God—and fasting and prayer (Acts 13:1-3), what relationship is there, if any, between fellowship and prophecy? Luke points to the importance of fellowship as the essential substratum of that very first church (Acts 2:42), before elaborating on the specific, foundational importance of prophets to the church at Antioch (Acts 13:1-3). Paul agrees that the church is built upon prophets and apostles (Eph. 2:20), but were the giftings of such people dependent firstly upon the existence of (spiritual) bonds of partnership, such as would have been engendered by the shared missions to the Gentiles? Our own later participation in small groups seemed to mirror this prophet based structure, and Chris would regularly receive and share a word with the rest of the group, stimulating further prayer and revelation in the other group members. Invariably, the small prayer groups to which we belonged were composed largely of women, who, because they are generally more available during the daytime, can spend the necessary time together developing intimacy with each other. Women do, however, seem always to have a head start on men when it comes to fellowshipping, and this focuses attention once again upon participation (Gk.—*koinonia*) in shared or common experience. Once such a level of intimacy has been achieved within a small group, the resident prophet(s) can operate in a completely uninhibited manner, receiving the initial word for the 'body' as a whole to craft into shape. Another function of the prophet within such groups is to help coordinate and synthesize the various prayers (monologues) and revelations into a productive dialogue with God. The prophet thus becomes a (dialogical) resource for God's people within the fellowship bonds of the small group, and this suggests that prophets should be identified as such at an early stage in fellowship group formation.

Christian prophets do not appear to figure much in Luke's account of the early church until, that is, after the first great persecution recorded in Acts 8:1. The early fellowship bonds formed after Pentecost would, no doubt, be strengthened further through the sharing of the adversities and afflictions of that persecution. It is widely accepted that Luke addresses a geographical agenda in his account of the formation of the early Christian Church, when he writes in Acts 1:8: "You will be my witnesses in Jerusalem, in all Judea and Samaria, and to the ends of the earth." Nevertheless, his record can be relied upon as being chronologically accurate and sequential, at least in regard to the post-Pentecost formation of strongly bonded, intimate groups of believers. Moreover the appearance of Christian prophets is not found until fairly late in Luke's account (Acts 11:27; 13:1), and appears to follow directly from the great persecution after Stephen's death (Acts 11:19). It would, therefore, seem safe to conclude that the gifting, identification, and recognition of Christian prophets as such, took place within those scattered, 'closely knit' groups and that this might be a template for the 'raising up' of our own prophets. Perhaps it is in this process that depression, aggravated by fasting, plays a part, serving to distinguish group members who are particularly gifted as prophets, and whose strong ties of fellowship allow them to share in confidence "in proportion to faith." Thus, a paradox is revealed in which fellowship ties originally born of "the breaking of bread" (Acts 2:42), and supplemented by the mutual experience of hard times, may enable groups to fast together to corporately receive and compositely craft a word from God.

A personal illustration of just how important it is to forge strong fellowship bonds before engaging in prayer-dialogue, occurred recently in a session of an ecumenical, healing prayer group to which Chris and I belonged. The group had been formed originally from at least five churches (three denominations) within the town, and initially numbered about fourteen. Two or three members were quickly lost when their church leaders instructed them (yes—this still happens!) to leave the group, but the remainder continued to meet together on a monthly basis. These meetings were soon supplemented by bimonthly healing services in one of the remaining three churches, and also eventually by biannual 'socials.' The net result was that the 'contact time' of the group members with each other, probably amounted to an average of three hours monthly. The group considered that it needed a 'spiritual director,' and it was agreed that this should be the leader of one of the churches who would attend meetings as frequently as his other duties permitted. During this particular prayer session, which occurred a full two years on from the group's inception, the objective had been to seek the LORD's guidance for the future direction of the group's activities. In the silence I received a vision. Now this in itself was unusual because although I do receive visions from time to time, I almost always do so in a subsidiary, supporting role and it is normally Chris who receives an initial word of scripture. Chris remained silent, however, as did the others and I felt it was up to me to share my vision, which I have to admit was the outcome of a sleepy reverie seemingly brought on by the quietness. Falling asleep in prayer meetings is probably not to be recommended as a general rule, but I believe there is scriptural precedent (see chapter 12–Jonah) for the hypnopompic, altered state of consciousness into which I fell. For no apparent reason I had envisioned the reed boat in which Moses had been set adrift on the river Nile shortly after his birth. My vision of the scene differed, however, from the original scriptural context in that there were *two* babies in the coracle, and upon reluctantly sharing this picture, our 'spiritual director' pronounced that in the Exodus record only one baby, Moses, was in the boat! Well precisely! My receipt of a picture rather than Chris's receipt of a verse had, I suspect, been precisely to avoid thrusting the group into scriptural contexts, and it was intended to concentrate the group's attention on the *current context*—that of seeking direction for the group from the LORD. Deflated and with my confidence evaporated, I could only prophesy "in proportion to (my) faith," so I left it to the group to discuss or pray it through further, even though I knew something of what the LORD wanted to convey. The clear intent of the vision—so far as I was concerned—was the depiction of the people of God (symbolized by Moses) split into two, and that this mirrored the denominational composition of our still infant fellowship group. Extended fellowship was a feature of both halves of the group, but *not* the group as a whole, and because such bonds were not in place intimate (spiritual) communication between us failed to transpire. The hypnopompic vision should have been the starting point for a longish, dialogue with the LORD, to develop and expand on what He wanted to convey to the group, but sadly, an opportunity was lost.

The Christian Prophet

The great persecution in Jerusalem starting on the day when Stephen died (Acts 8:1) is described using the Greek word, *diogmos*, which is translated in most English versions of the bible as 'persecution,' but which can carry the principle meaning of 'chase' or 'pursue.' When Luke comes to recounting the longer term aftermath of those events in Acts 11:19, he uses a different word (Greek, *thlipsis*), which is again translated into English as 'persecution.' But the significance of this word for Luke lies in its connections with the effects of crushing repression, exemplified by the imprisonments in Jerusalem. The incarcerations of Acts 8:3 should be compared with Acts 7:10 where the reference is to Genesis 41:14, in which Joseph is rescued from all his afflictions (Greek, *thlipsis*), and Genesis 42:21 where Joseph and his brothers suffer 'anguish of soul' (Greek, *thlipsis*). Thus, the result of such repression was probably the same for all the Christians, both the prisoners and their loved ones—despairing black depression, and it is this internal psychological condition, also associated with semi-starvation (Acts 7:11), which this word often alludes to. Paul enlightens us further when he uses the same word (2 Cor. 7:5) to describe the result of both outside repression and internal fears. The nascent Christian church, forced into a new diaspora following Stephen's death would, as a consequence, have amongst its number many who were familiar with depression. Parallels now become apparent between these depressed Christians and the known depressives (Moses, Elijah, Jonah) in the Old Testament. Moreover, it will be seen that the circumstances of despairing national melancholy that prevailed in the immediate aftermath of the exile, and which led to the 'raising up' of Jeremiah, Ezekiel, and Daniel, are comparable.

Given that Paul is clear in his insistence that "all may prophesy," (1 Cor. 14:31) and having already suggested that fasting is a possible means of discovering those with prophetic giftings, I am bound to wonder whether those who were *recognized* as prophets were, or had been, subject to rather more prolonged depressions borne of adversity. This may be posed in a rather more colloquial manner as the question: Is it necessary for a Christian to 'go through hell and back' in order to become (recognized as) a prophet? I believe so, and indeed consider that the 'psychiatric illness' that Chris endured was precisely such a process, and one that Paul, himself, may also have endured (Col. 1:24; 2 Cor. 12:7). Certainly, the word used by Luke to describe internal psychological affliction (Gk.—*thlipsis* Acts 7:10, 11) is once again present in Colossians 1:24 and the other verses in which Paul talks of his personal sufferings (Rom. 5:3; 2 Cor. 4:17; 7:4–5; 1 Thess. 1:6). Again using the same Greek word, *thlipsis* (translated once again as 'persecution' in later English versions!), Luke encapsulates the relationship between internal psychological suffering and experiencing the things of the Spirit in Acts 14:22:

> Confirming the souls of the disciples, and exhorting them to continue in the faith, and that we must through much tribulation enter into the kingdom of God. (Acts 14:22 KJV).

Where their modern counterparts have used the word 'persecution,' the translators of the Authorized Version have used the much older and far more descriptive word 'tribulation'—a word that has now more or less passed into disuse. In its original Latin setting, however, 'tribulation' refers to enormous crushing pressure, such as would have been applied to wheat on the threshing floor using a heavy threshing sledge (Latin, *tribulum*). This scenario of being pressed down will be readily recognized by all those who have ever suffered from depression, and who when momentarily freed from it, talk about 'a huge weight having been lifted from them.' Paul's words concerning his own personal sufferings in Colossians 1:24 have puzzled translators and commentators over the years, but his (in)famous "thorn in the flesh" (2 Cor. 12:7) which was certainly of a spiritual nature, is to be found in a context of Ezekiel like prophetic activity. Paul's language here is reminiscent of Galatians 4:13–15 where his preaching is said to be the direct result of an "infirmity of the flesh" (Gal. 4:13 KJV). Unfortunately, the rather old fashioned word 'flesh' is all too easily associated with the physical body in the minds of modern readers, and these phrases, "infirmity of/thorn in the flesh" might more profitably be read with Gordon Fee as 'an irritating weakness of (my) humanness, or creatureliness.' If that 'infirmity' was of a depressive nature, it would help to explain Paul's suicidal musings recorded in Philippians 1:20–23:

> If I am to go on living in the body, this will mean fruitful labor
> for me. Yet what shall I choose? I do not know!
> I am torn between the two: I desire to depart and be with Christ,
> which is better by far; (Phil. 1:22–23 NIV)

In a manner reminiscent of Moses (Num. 11:15) and Elijah (1 Kings 19:4), Paul is here expressing a desire to have his life terminated and moreover, that this lies within his own choice, and dare one say, with his LORD's agreement! Paul is venerated both for the profound theological insights in his writings and the clarity with which his letters are constructed. Such lucidity is a known function of depressives who achieve their utmost creativity during their darkest moments, and whose ranks have included many of the world's finest poets, artists, and musicians. Tchaikovsky's black despair during his composition of "The Nutcracker Suite" is to give just one example from among many. Chris's best letters were written (and her best paintings painted) during her darkest days, and are the tangible artefacts that testify to her suicidal longings. Chris, like Paul before her, found herself compelled to endure sufferings, which the LORD would not take away, and which were endured simultaneously with Jesus himself. It may be observed with James Dunn that "Christ's sufferings are incomplete until the last suffering of the last Christian," and this is perhaps the salutary and irreducible lesson that all Christians need to learn again.

16

My Burden is Light

Upon our return from holiday in Turkey, I had recuperated to some extent from the exhaustion of my final year at bible college, and I felt it was necessary to take stock of our situation. Chris, although managing to do about four hours of voluntary work a week, was still unable to contemplate longer periods of paid employment, and the voluntary work was more in the nature of personal therapy for her than anything else. I was now fifty three years old and having spent something over five years as a full time carer for Chris, I knew I would struggle if I were to go back into a 'normal' work environment again. Besides, even though a qualified, yet inexperienced teacher of two shortage subjects, I had no desire to enter an education system that expelled twelve thousand children a year, simply because it had no other disciplinary sanctions. I thought that I might be a 'good teacher' if only because during a Christian 'retreat weekend' in the Lake District, I had completed one of those spiritual giftings questionnaires—beloved of charismatics, finding that I was apparently equally gifted as a pastor and a teacher. Later on I discovered that when Paul uses the phrase "pastors and teachers" in Ephesians 4:11, he is expressing a single, complex idea known technically as a *hendiadys*. This single, complex idea conveys a totally different concept to that of either term, which are normally considered to be quite separate by modern Christians, and is much more suited to the informal, peripatetic teaching environments typical of Paul's Asia Minor. If indeed

I was (spiritually) gifted in this way, it was not a skill that could be easily utilized within the increasingly regulated state education system.

It was good to be cool again after the heat of Turkey and we were able to take short walks in the fresher, English sunshine, mulling over our options as we did so, and it was during one such rather beautiful afternoon that we were joined on our walk by a college friend. Our friend, who I shall call John, had yet to complete his fourth and final year at college, but this had not prevented him from accepting the (unpaid) position of pastor with a tiny inner city fellowship. As we walked, he gave us some background information about the church and about his decision to pastor it, and suggested that we might like to join him in this enterprise! As we strolled in the breeze amid birdsong and flowers, the very idea of spending time, quite a lot of time, at an inner city church appalled us, and of course we said the usual thing that Christians' say in such circumstances—we'll pray about it! Now praying is a real problem when you have a prophet around, because one tends to get answers, and usually pretty unequivocal ones at that, and this occasion was typical. We were quickly assured that the LORD wanted us involved and this was confirmed a week or so later, when at the end of a short break in the Yorkshire Dales, Chris received a couple of (fairly rare) New Testament verses. I did not record these verses, but in essence they compared us with Paul as he set out on one or other of his missions, and it was clear that we were to be apostles, if only for one year. It seemed to make good sense from purely human considerations too, since I was unsure whether the MA course that I was hoping to join in the following January would run, and it seemed that our friend needed help, particularly in this, his final examination year. So it was then, that we began a strange and in many respects bizarre period in our lives, during which we benefited immensely from our new, yet temporary apostolic role.

Mission

Although we had agreed to help and support John, it was quite clear from the outset that the time we could spend with the fellowship was limited, if only because the church was such a long way away from home. The long hours of commuting—frequently late at night—were to eventually become a serious drain on Chris's still impaired health. So a pattern developed in which we would go down about twice a week, once on Sunday mornings—often staying late into the afternoon—and also on Tuesday evenings. The Tuesday evening meeting also met in the church building and effectively corresponded to a home fellowship group, except in this case it numbered twelve as a maximum and comprised the whole church. Fellowship indeed there was, however, and there were few occasions when a pork pie supper was not served! The format of the meeting followed the fairly typical praise, bible study, and prayer sequence, and I undertook the preparation of the bible studies to reduce the pastor's workload. What was not too typical, however, were the circumstances under which these fellowship meetings took place, and by way of explanation it is necessary to describe this inner city locale in greater detail. The church building was a fairly modern, brick-built, single-storey affair, situated adjacent to a health centre and close to a small group of shops, and it was quite the most alien environment we had ever spent time in. It was bizarre—the fish and chip shop had ram raid defences, the fire brigade were pelted with stones as they attended purposely set fires, and the police helicopter never left the night sky. Cars, including police cars, could not be left by the roadside, because they would be quite literally destroyed, and to avoid theft the local council carried out all its municipal works in the mornings, since that was when the local 'children' slept!' The church building itself was fortified with barbed wire all around the roof, strong polycarbonate windows, and steel-plated doors, and in our first few weeks there, the church sanctuary was ram raided with a stolen car. Our Tuesday evenings would commence with the parking of our own vehicle, which had to be done on the driveway of an adjacent council house (the rationale being that vehicles that were seen 'to belong' to locals were left unharmed), before we joined our friends inside the church.

After the first few meetings it soon became apparent to us that one of the principle reasons for our being there was prayer, and that this broke down into three main areas. We would pray regularly with the Tuesday evening fellowship group about the local area, and this was supplemented by our own prayer times at home on the same topic. Thirdly, there was to be a regular, weekly prayer session with our pastor friend, which would take place either at the church or at our home, so that each of us could take turns to do the travelling. It has to be said that many of those early Tuesday evening sessions were often a complete shambles from beginning to end. Firstly, it took about forty five minutes to get everybody there for what should have been a seven o'clock start, and this would be followed by a 'cup of tea' lasting a further half hour. When everyone had finally settled down the praise songs would begin, but so too would the 'bombardment,' as the plastic windows and steel doors were pounded with half bricks! After twenty minutes or so the noise would stop and a little knocking would come on the outside door, which when opened revealed perhaps a half dozen 'children.' I place quotation marks around the word 'children' advisedly, because in truth usually only one of them could be so described. In any event, the pastor always welcomed them inside on the basis that given enough exposure to 'The Word,' they would eventually respond and be 'saved.' Sadly, his genuine, touching benevolence was in the main misdirected, and the majority of them displayed what can only be described as a united, malevolent, *spiritual* antipathy towards the fellowship group, which utterly disrupted the meeting and invariably brought it to an early close. The only way to counter the spiritual oppression, which lay over the entire locality in general, and was manifested through these malevolent 'fifth columnists' in particular, was to attack them spiritually, that is, to pray!

In the main, neither the fellowship nor the pastor fully understood the spiritual nature of the thorough going battle we were all engaged in, and the prayers which should have been a regular feature of the church's life under such circumstances were erratic. Our scheduled prayer meetings with the pastor soon began to suffer postponements and cancellations, before finally ceasing altogether. Sadly, John appeared to fall into the trap of relying on his undoubted human abilities, rather than using prayer to direct and apply raw spiritual power to the problems of the area. As with any military endeavor, the direction of prayer as a weapon against spiritual evil depends upon good intelligence gathering, and to do this in a spiritual situation requires the deployment of prophets. In this regard the church was inordinately blessed, since in addition to Chris we found that the pastor's wife had similar prophetic giftings. From the start, what should have been a battle with 'principalities and powers,' turned into an endless round of coffee mornings, drop-ins, inter-church socials, and impromptu youth groups, all of which finally brought the handful of helpers (including the pastor and his wife) to the brink of exhaustion. All that we could do was pray ourselves, but it took some weeks before the regular need for this impressed itself on us, yet when we finally got down to it, we found that our Tuesday evenings became times of relative peace and tranquillity. Outside the building the battle continued to rage through the winter months, with fires being set alight both against the church walls and also inside the empty terraced houses in the adjacent street. Then, during one particular Sunday, prayer-dialogue session we made a breakthrough.

It transpired that during the previous (C19th) century this whole inner city area had been developed into a docks and warehousing complex by one man in particular, and a man whom I had come to know of in a different capacity. Indeed, I knew that this man had been a member of the same 'fraternal fellowship' to which I had belonged, and had moreover, been the founder of a 'lodge' that still carries his name. Now it is a well known fact that the upper echelons of this brotherhood—to which this man belonged by reason of his rank—have access to occult knowledge. It was this occult association (whether actively indulged in or not) that underpinned the great pall of spiritual oppression that lay over the area, and having once established this it was a simple matter to pray appropriate remedial prayers. The effect was instantaneous! Over the remainder of that Sunday afternoon, Chris received 'word' after 'word' from the LORD, who was clearly in paroxysms of delight over the day's actions. The 'acid test,' however, would and did come over the following weeks and months, as the area slowly yet progressively quietened down, and a quite unnerving peace seemed to settle over the area. No more fires were set, not even on the following November 5th! The adjacent street which had been the scene of so much trouble, and which also carried the name of the lodge founding 'brother,' was eventually pulled down, and the marauding gangs of youths slowly dissipated. Now that the external situation had been dealt with, the only threat to harmony within the church lay in the continued mentoring of that same small group of disruptive youths by the pastor. This unilateral action on the part of the pastor was not supported by the rest of the fellowship, and was eventually to drive a wedge between them.

Failure

Fairly early on in our association with the church we were asked to become joint treasurers by the church board, which is a rather grand sounding title for what was effectively three quarters of the fellowship. The appointment as joint treasurers was due to the ill health of the existing treasurer, and the absence of anyone else with either the ability or inclination to take the job on. But it was less than an ideal situation from the outset, if only because the relative infrequency of our visits inevitably caused delays in dealing with financial matters. On the face of it, Chris was the perfect candidate, given the bookkeeping and administrative skills she had acquired during our business partnership days. I warned, however, that if Chris were to suffer even a slight deterioration in her generally poor health, then things could easily get out of hand. In the event Chris's health remained relatively good throughout the first twelve months, but began to worsen gradually over the ensuing months. Of course our original 'commission' from the LORD had been for twelve months only, despite the pastor's clear belief and expectation that we would eventually follow his example and set up home in the area. Naturally, we prayed about the situation, only to learn that we should continue as 'caretaker' treasurers for a further interim period until a successor was found, but that our original apostolic and prophetic functions here were at an end.

By this time, Chris's worsening health was causing a significant fall off in the frequency of our visits, and sadly this contributed to an acrimonious parting with our friends during a general meeting of the church held in the July of that second summer. As I ruefully ruled off the accounts and prepared to return the books, I pondered on the events of the previous twenty two months coming to the conclusion that it had all been a dismal failure. Certainly in superficial human terms we had helped preside over the death throes of just another ailing, inner city church, and it would be easy to label it as yet another casualty of the 'post Christian era,' but would such an assessment be accurate? Indeed, what were our conversations with God telling us? Throughout those final months of schism, the LORD was continuing to say that He would always have a presence in that building in that locality, but that it would not continue to be led by our friend. At a special service in the autumn of that final year we were able to see the building handed over to a strange, new fellowship, which seemed at first sight to be composed of characters that were more terrifying than the old neighborhood gangs. In the main, these young Christians who came complete with shaved heads and ear rings, were truly 'born again' from their past lives as criminals and drug addicts, and *they prayed*, they prayed all the time, boy how they prayed! It seemed from our dialogues with the LORD that we had fulfilled a baton carrying role, and therefore we had contributed to the maintenance of a Christian presence in the neighborhood in the form of this successor church. If indeed, there had been failure it had not been on our part, and the same prophetic insights that had identified the problems, were now telling us that our time there had been a great success. God, it seems, is satisfied with so little—his burden is indeed light!

The Vision

As already mentioned in chapter eleven, our conversations with the LORD seemed to gather momentum from about the beginning of 1999, and were positively in 'hyper drive' by the time we had returned from Turkey that summer. The initiation of these dialogues was frequently by the LORD himself and the single theme of 'The Day of the LORD' would constantly emerge. It seemed that we were privy to knowledge about an impending, modern 'Day of the LORD,' which was soon to engulf the world, a 'Day' in which social, political, and economic turmoil would manifest itself on a hitherto unprecedented scale. Occasionally we were asked to pray, but normally we were just party to the information, which we were not required (i.e. burdened) to share with anyone. We believed this was going to happen not because of the advancing year end with its expected 'millennium bug,' computer crashes, or the astrological predictions of disaster associated with the 1999 eclipse, but because the LORD had told us so, time after time after time. It was a reality to us, so much so, that we began to stockpile food, fuel, and other essentials, and we could not avoid sharing our knowledge with our friends—John included.

By the time our inner city mission began, John had completely appropriated what we had been saying, and when he received independent corroboration in the December, his response was immediate. That confirmation had come in the form of a newsletter, which he along with about two hundred other pastors had received in the post. The newsletter had been sent by a small group of independent, black African churches, which had banded themselves together under the banner 'Intercessory Action Group.' Their group had been incepted after a vision had been given to one of their number earlier in the year, and in faith they had mounted a campaign to galvanize the city's church leaders into action. The vision contained some pretty terrifying stuff, but in a nutshell it depicted the coming of the LORD as a huge fireball that would destroy the moribund Western Christian Church. Our friend's response had been to make the church building available to the group for any subsequently organized meeting of pastors, since at a push it could seat about one hundred and squeeze others in standing. A first meeting was arranged in early December, and was both disappointing and humbling. It was disappointing because there were only about eighteen of us, eight or nine of whom were the leaders of churches. It was humbling because most of those pastors were Africans—the progeny of Victorian Christian missions—yet here they were, earnestly and sincerely interceding for the church and people of a major city in Northern England. If Chris's prophetic insights had been about the larger world picture, the group's 'brief' had been about one nation in particular, and was specific to the church of that nation beginning with the city that was their home.

The first meeting was followed by others, all of them being dominated by the group's repeated and earnest plea that the LORD should relent, and it came as a surprise to find out that Chris had, for some time, also been asking the LORD to relent of his terrible intentions. In the event, the group's fervent supplications were successful, at least partially so, and we learned that the LORD was 'withholding his arm,' the net effect of which was to both reduce and delay those intended actions. If the intention of prayer is to change the things that have not yet come to be then we were indeed successful, and the rumblings and tremors within the global financial markets did not develop to any significant extent in that 'millennium' year. The politicians and the media resisted talk of a 'slow down' in the world economy as the year end came, and steadfastly refused to use the R (recession) word throughout the following spring! But the steady slide in financial markets continued for a full year, before that infamous day, henceforth to be known simply and for always as 9/11 changed everything. Until then I had believed that the impending 'Day of the LORD' was to be almost entirely an onslaught against financial markets, with clear economic, social, and of course spiritual consequences flowing from that. I had not, however, allowed for the fact that our God operates on a multifactorial basis, or to put it another way, He rarely does only one thing at once.

But what am I saying here? Is God responsible for the events of September 11th? The answer is yes, probably, and I know I am opening Pandora's box by suggesting this, but it is an entirely scriptural understanding of the nature and character of God. In order to reach such a conclusion certain precepts must be accepted, not the least of which is accepting that God is active in the world now and has been throughout history. Secondly, the existence of spiritual forces opposed to God's purposes must be a given, and that man himself as a spiritual entity can be the agent of these forces. In such circumstances the latter agency may triumph especially when God withholds his protection, as was so frequently the case with pre-exilic Israel. On the other hand, one could say that September 11th was always ever going to happen given the global politics of our time, and that in this case the free will of a group of determined terrorists prevailed. But does this mean that God's plans can be thwarted? Can He lose? The answer again is yes, probably. I keep using the word 'probably' because probability, chance, and uncertainty are factors, which are intimately bound up, in divine planning and actions. In this respect, it is interesting to reflect that amongst the words we received concerning the 'Day of the LORD,' was the following verse from Isaiah:

> I will deliver the Egyptians into the hand of a hard master; a fierce king will rule over them, says the Sovereign, the LORD of hosts. (Is. 19:4 NRSV)

This verse was given several times in response to our questions about the extremely close and hotly disputed outcome of the American presidential election, and has nothing to do with Egyptians in the modern, post cold war context, save to say that they may be representative Moslems. It simply means that a new leader of the single, remaining, modern superpower will emerge (analogous to Assyria in the Old Testament context), and he will be hard. So, it may not be too simplistic to say that whereas the previous presidency had aided Moslems against Christians (Kosovo), the new administration would begin to prosecute a relentless war against hard line Islam in

Afganistan, Palestine (by proxy), and finally in Iraq. The issue here is war, not so much against terrorism, as against the ideology or rather philosophy of a hard line and unforgiving Islam that uses terrorism to achieve its ends, and interestingly, that war is being prosecuted by spiritual forces using the world's only remaining superpower as agent. As I write these words the feudal government of Saudi Arabia maintains its adopted Western philosophy in the face of a ferment of internal opposition from Islamic fundamentalists, and just across the Gulf the Iranians continue with their plans to develop nuclear weapons. American, British, and European leaders meet to thwart those plans by diplomatic means, but is it only a matter of time before a new American expeditionary force sets out for Persia? On the world's financial markets, the bear market on the world's stock exchanges appears to be over, yet the 'rebound' in stock values appears to be unusually sluggish. The battle lines in this war are not simply drawn over the price of oil as so many (green) commentators would have us believe, but rather between two philosophies—neither of which give glory to God. The world it seems is poised precariously on the brink of harrowing times, holding its breath as it awaits developments.

17

In the Cool of the Day

IN THIS FINAL CHAPTER I will attempt to draw out some general conclusions from our personal journey of the last ten years, and which I believe might have wider applicability to the way in which Christians practise their faith today. Perhaps the first thing to note should be that our Christian walk began not with mountain top experiences, but in the crushing black despair of a life and livelihood destroyed through unremitting 'psychiatric illness.' Once again I place quotation marks around these two words because they encapsulate an entire worldview, and moreover, one that I believe is diametrically opposed to that found in scripture. It is the all pervading nature of this current world view which evokes such a violent response from militant Islam, which motivates the empty, secular Judaism of modern Israel, and which is choking the (Western) Christian church to death at the birth of this third millennium. Leaders of all these world religions find themselves either drawn into opposing world secularism or compelled to endorse it, and that endorsement is exemplified by the new idols they find themselves inadvertently worshipping. In Britain, the world famous National Health Service (NHS) has become such an idol, and politicians of all parties espouse the need to fund the NHS at the rate of ten percent of the national budget. This it is argued will bring Britain into line with other European states who *tithe* to their god on a similar scale! As a consequence, politicians and the people who elect them, have been fully convinced by a medical view of man that sees depression as an 'illness' to be treated, rather than a feature or trait of our very humanity.

Illness of any kind tends to express or push people to the outer fringes of modern society, if only because our partnerships (livelihoods or economies–Greek, *koinonia*) now derive in the main from outside our families. Those classified as psychiatrically 'ill' are likewise expelled from society, even church society, and this is especially so with depression because of its long term nature. So instead of depressives being full members of churches—as originally based on small (family) households—they are now sent to a place of isolation, which in the modern world can be either the home or the psychiatric ward of a hospital. The shift of power, both political and economic, away from families has left the church without communicative access to God through its prophets, who as with Paul, derive their ability from their gifting, that is, through depression:

> and He said to me, 'Sufficient for thee is My grace, for My power in infirmity is perfected;' most gladly, therefore, will I rather boast in my infirmities, that the power of the Christ may rest on me: (2 Corinthians 12:9, Young's Literal Translation)

According to Jesus, the power of God is perfected, that is, is at its strongest in weakness, infirmity or 'illness,' yet we modern Christians meet in church buildings, leaving our 'sick' brothers at home! Before attempting to draw out the implications of this for the future of the Christian church, and having labelled Paul as a depressive, it would seem appropriate to deal firstly with the apparent inconsistency presented by Paul's obvious joy.

Christian Joy

From the earliest days of my Christian commitment, I had always had great difficulty with one particular fruit of the Spirit, that is, with Christian joy, but after these years of dialogue with the LORD with and through Chris, I have come to understand that this really means intimacy with God. Paul exemplifies the Spirit filled Christian prophet who is at once filled with joy, yet remains pervaded by a crushed brokenness that is clearly consistent with depression. What then is this Christian joy that Paul shares with the Thessalonians? In the Greek of 1 Thessalonians 1:6 we once again find the word *thlipsis*, which the translators seem utterly at odds over:

> And ye became followers of us, and of the Lord, having received the word in much affliction, with joy of the Holy Ghost: (1 Thess. 1:6 KJV)

The translators of the King James Version elect for affliction as do those of the RSV, whilst some later English versions choose suffering (NIV) or persecution (NRSV), and the Young's Literal Translation favors tribulation following the Latin. What most translators do agree on is that the Thessalonians became imitators of Paul and his friends rather than followers, as the KJV would have it. But does that mean that the Thessalonians deliberately sought (external) persecution or suffering in order to imitate Paul? I think not, and one is compelled towards the understanding that (at least some of) the Thessalonians are imitating Paul in their sharing of the same internal psychological condition, whether by virtue of being innately depressed or by cultivating that condition through fasting. What seems clear is that (some of?) the Thessalonians underwent tribulation, that is, they were crushed, and that they received 'the word' either via Paul or more likely directly from the LORD inside (Greek, *en*) or because of that condition. Moreover, this happened at the same time as being filled with joy by the Holy Spirit, and one is compelled to conclude that black, crushing despair is coexisting simultaneously here with unspeakable joy! Such a description might seem at first sight to accord well with the medical condition known as manic depression, but that would be wrong because there are no swings in mood here between highs and lows, rather the two conditions, joy and depression coexist together. This is certainly what came out of my many discussions with Chris, who would describe how she underwent long periods of ecstatic elation, which corresponded exactly with her blackest moments.

Imitators of Christ?

Ancient Mediterranean societies (ethnic or people groups) were made up of large extended families and the societal pressures on such families could be immense. The adoption of an 'alien' belief system within such a close knit community would without doubt engender controversy, with the result that any societal lines of schism would propagate internal fissures within individual families. A small Christian community living within such a closely bonded, corporate society, would undoubtedly experience ostracism, that is, a very public banishment or 'sending to Coventry.' The effects of such dissension upon individual members of families, would without doubt involve the breaking of close family bonds of relationship, leading to severe, internal psychological problems—effectively threatening the person's very identity. Such problems would almost certainly manifest themselves as depression, brought about directly by the external persecution noted by Paul in 1 Thess. 2:14. It has to be remembered that this is a corporate society not long removed from its tribal roots, in which the concept of 'the individual' is an alien one, and in which one's very identity depends upon being firmly fixed within a familial matrix. So then, quite apart from the physical effects of a schism within the community, such as violence or the withholding of scarce, shared resources, there would be internal psychological pressure bearing down on (some) members of families. The outworking of this pressure would be depression, and this accounts for the great breadth of meaning attributed to the Greek word, *thlipsis*, (i.e. affliction, tribulation, suffering, persecution etc.) permitting Paul to say:

> For even when we came into Macedonia, our bodies had no rest, but we were afflicted in every way—disputes without and fears within. (2 Cor. 7:5 NSRV)

Depression then is 'part and parcel' of persecution in such a strongly bonded corporate society, indeed, it might not be putting it too strongly to suggest that depression would be largely absent from such a society, *except* where persecution forced a breakdown in the familial matrix. This point may be pushed a little further by suggesting that the depression suffered by more than ten percent of modern Western 'individuals,' may directly result from the near *absence* of such a comprehensive familial matrix in much of (persecution free) Western society.

Paul's assertion that the Thessalonians became "imitators of us, *and* of the LORD, having received the word in much tribulation," would seem somewhat odd at first sight, given that the gospel writers never actually applied the word 'tribulation' to Jesus himself. In a more literal translation of the Greek the comparison of the Thessalonians with Jesus (1 Thess. 1:6) becomes even clearer:

> and ye—ye did become imitators of us, and of the Lord, being receivers of the word in much tribulation, with joy of the Holy Spirit, (1 Thess. 1:6)

What then did Jesus share with the Thessalonians? It could only be the breakdown of his own familial and ethnic bonds with resultant psychological consequences, consequences that may very well continue in eternity. Thus, Paul is not so much exhorting people to become like him or Jesus, as acknowledging that those who do should embrace both the advantages and disadvantages of the condition. Put simply, the joy of a communicating, personal relationship with God is likely to be concurrent with crushing brokenness.

"Let the Dead Bury the Dead"

The schisms in both the Thessalonian and Judean communities were not unanticipated, and the separation of Christian believers from their kith and kin was even foretold by John the Baptist, who considered it to be a function of the Holy Spirit (Matt. 3:11). When John speaks of the later baptism with 'Holy Spirit and fire,' he is using a foundational metaphor that pervades the writings of the Old Testament prophets. The allusion in this metaphor is to the end times salvation of remnant Israel in terms of the air and fire refining of silver from lead/silver alloy—a theme that is frequently found in the prophets (e.g. Zec. 13:9; Mal. 3:3). Silver is just one product of the refining process underlying this metaphor, the other product being a form of lead oxide, which although useful, is of far less value than silver. This smithing process causes the silver to be *separated, purified,* and *saved,* and it therefore symbolizes a like process applied to remnant Israel in which the sinful bonds between the world and the elect are broken. The full force of the analogy lies in the conditions of the separation, which are the same for humans as they are for metals, that is, fierce heat made all the hotter by the Breath of God! Once separated, the two metals never again become metallurgically bonded together, and in the same way once the righteous (silver) have been separated from the unrighteous, they can never be allowed to rebond to each other. Unfortunately, although this metaphor exactly depicts the separation process, it has nothing to say about the painful psychological consequences of such a separation for the people involved.

By the time of Jesus, six hundred plus years of prophetic insights had conveyed this message of separation to the people of Israel, who, in the main misinterpreted it, looking instead for a military means to separate them from their conquerors. So when Jesus said to one of his disciples: "Follow me, and let the dead bury their own dead." (Matt. 8:22), he was making it almost brutally plain that the boundaries of the Kingdom of God run right through the middle of families. This may be paraphrased to read: "Let those who are not in relationship with me (God) look after those who are not in relationship with me." Thus, by implication Jesus was also saying: "But as for you follow, or remain in relationship with me, and *I* will look after you." The saying is therefore a variation of Jesus' first commandment—to love (prefer the interests of) God above all others. It is interesting to note that the following verse (Matt. 8:23) appears to have been inserted precisely to convey the decision of the disciple in question, however much pain that choice caused him. Jesus then, is not so much endorsing the schisms later found in both the Thessalonian and Judean communities, as making it plain that they are normal for Christians. It is a supreme paradox that the very act of separation in this way can effect an internal psychological condition, which engenders, facilitates, and enhances a communicating relationship with God. The modern medical 'label' for this internal psychological state is depression, but in ancient times it was quite simply considered to be just one aspect of what it means to be human. Separation by death is the common experience of human beings and the act of mourning the dead is known to lead to reactive depression, but mourning and fasting following death or separation are used as synonyms by Matthew (Matt. 9:15) indicating that the relationship of these terms can only be via depression. The result of depression, however brought about, was seen to be the same—a dialogical relationship with God, and I would suggest that the difference between a 'prophet' and 'one who prophesies' is related only to the severity of the depression endured.

The Death of a Friend

I hope I have made it plain throughout this book that in scripture, depression—whether mild or severe, is an underlying, characteristic feature of the human condition, which for whatever reason, lends itself to prophetic gifting. I have also remarked that severe depression leading to successful suicides occurs much less frequently in scripture than in other writings of antiquity, and that this can only be the result of divine intervention. How then, in light of this, is one to understand the death of Christians by suicide? The question became one of personal significance when we were notified of the death by suicide of a dear friend, Anne—one of the original prayer group members who had helped Chris through her blackist time. It was such a perverse paradox to find ourselves attending the funeral of our Christian friend, one who with prayer and the laying on of hands had been so central to preventing Chris from taking her own life. In Anne's case the severity of her depression had led to death, and this raises the question of why this should happen in her case, but not in the case of (the majority of?) other Christians?

Looking back, it seems that the story began at the time of the church split, when the members of the prayer group were forbidden to associate with us, and they themselves were equally split down the middle regarding Chris's prophetic manifestations. Two members of the group, including Anne, simply could not accept the whole plethora of prophetic attributes Chris now possessed. Moreover, at about this time, dramatic changes began to take place in Anne's life, which had hitherto been largely dominated by the roles of wife and mother to four children. A career move involving

Sunday working began to diminish the opportunities available to her for Christian fellowship, and estrangement and separation from her husband followed soon after. The combination of Sunday working, the split with her friends in the prayer group, marital separation, and reduced access to children (who had remained in the parental home), had within a very few years utterly destroyed Anne's supporting familial matrix. Everything that defined her *identity* had gone leaving her completely alone, and depression gradually ensued. Anne fled to a remote Greek island where the tourist-free winter months brought about even more isolation—this time due to language difficulties—and the depression grew worse. But what of her personal relationship to God? Could, indeed did, God intervene? I confess I do not know, but I wonder whether her Jesus was trying to communicate with her in her blackest despair, finding his efforts limited by a (very) human refusal to accept the reality of dialogue with the Divine?

It may have been that Anne had failed to hear, if only because she had felt alarmed by, or afraid of the manifestations she had seen in Chris, all those years before. She, like Chris ten years earlier, had convinced herself that her 'grown up' family didn't really need her anymore, and the same deadly siren voices were there, insisting that "no one will miss me if I die etc. etc.." When the depression got really bad there was no one there for her, and no amount of contact by email can make up for that. News of Anne's death came through another member of that same prayer group, and at a time when Chris herself was again suffering badly from depression—the result of the gradual failure of her current drug regime. The funeral was a desperately harrowing affair, as each of four distraught teenagers gave individual eulogies for their mother, and we came away very upset, quietly asking ourselves some pretty deep questions about a Christian walk, which had ended this way. We returned home, and having regained the peace of our living room, we questioned the LORD about the events of the afternoon. Our questions went something along the lines of:

- What have you to say about this dreadfully painful experience we have all been through just now?
- Why should the person you used to save Chris die from the very same peril?
- What is the point of it all, that is, Chris's survival—due in part to our friend's intercession?

The answer to this and other similar questions was partially inscrutable, partially predictive, and came in the form of one of those rare New Testament verses:

> For this reason I remind you to fan into flame the gift of God, which is in you through the laying on of my hands. (2 Tim. 1:6 NIV)

This word was at once both a reminder of Anne's instrumentality in Chris's gifting, and an exhortation to use it, but above all it was a comment on the high price in sorrow paid for that gift. Significantly here, "the laying on of hands" was both the laying on of Anne's hands and the LORD's hands, and the word is a profound re-affirmation of the 'physical' presence and co-inherence of the Master in his servant. It was a salutary word, which placed Chris's recently reawakened inclinations to self-harm in a divine perspective.

Does Depression Help?

As I write these final words I am again reflecting on our situation, for nothing much seems to have changed—at least in human terms. We remain an older couple who are estranged from the workplace, with the result that we are no longer 'interesting people,' and because of this we have assumed a position on the fringe of our family, our community and our society. Chris's few residual ME symptoms are sufficiently severe to preclude an active social life, and although my own academic work is continuing in the form of doctoral research, it seems to be another step on a ladder to nowhere. Indeed, there doesn't seem to be a great deal of demand for newly qualified, sixty year old theologians! If our lives can be compared with a single day, then we are in the 'evening' of our lives, that is, in 'the cool of the day,' yet the LORD continues to tell us that we have a significant future ministry. Moreover, He continues to talk about us in Jeremian terms, that is, as a pot still being formed on the Potter's wheel. As a pot we've had some false starts—that's where a potter crushes a wobbly pot back into a lump and re-centralizes it on the wheel, before beginning to throw again. After a pot has been thrown there are a number of other processes such as paring, drying, biscuit firing, glazing, and glaze firing, before ever a pot can be *used*, so we must continue to trust, be patient and await our time, even though that time is paradoxically in 'the cool of the day!'

Our conversations with God are in effect a live commentary on our progression through the pot-making process, and after a while one begins to accept that one's life is an 'object' being worked on, but with the bizarre difference that in this case the Craftsman talks to his work! Over the years, those conversations have progressively developed from what were initially manifestations of a divinatory nature—manifestations which caused no end of consternation amongst our Christian friends, but which subsequently became a fully verbal discourse. But the question remains: Did depression assist in that long attenuated process? Indeed, does God make use of depression—seen as a function of what it means to be human, in order to enter into dialogue with his people? Through our experiences over these past fifteen years, I have come to believe that depression does represent a characteristic aspect of being human, which somehow facilitates dialogical access to God, although I don't know why this should be so! Moreover, I consider that both the Old and the New Testaments abound with examples of depressives, whose prophetic gifting is perfected in the depths of despairing black depression. It is via this 'weakness of the flesh' that God usually succeeds in gaining his peoples' attention, before going on to develop a fuller dialogical relationship with them. Perhaps it is time for Christians to abandon an alien medical view that says depression is an illness, whilst at the same time being ever cognisant of its life-threatening potential. Christians should hold their fellows who suffer in this way firmly within a matrix of relationship, since their predisposition towards prophecy, gives them the potential to become valuable resources for the body of Christ.

Father, I pray you: Can we have our prophets back please?

Authoritative Sources Consulted

American Psychiatric Association, *Diagnostic and Statistical Manual of Mental Disorders: DSM IV.* Washington, DC: The American Psychiatric Association, 2000.

Barnes, Trevor. *Dealing with Depression.* London: Vermillion, 1996.

Bartchy, S. Scott. *First-Century Slavery and 1 Corinthians 7:21.* Atlanta: Scholars, 1973.

Bech, Per "Symptoms & Assessment of Depression." In *Handbook of Affective Disorders,* edited by Eugene S. Paykel, 3-13. Edinburgh: Churchill Livingstone, 1992.

Best, Ernest. *The 1st and 2nd Epistles to the Thessalonians.* London: A & C Black, 1972.

Brown, Colin ed. *The New International Dictionary of New Testament Theology Vol III.* Exeter: Paternoster, 1978.

Bruce, F. F. *Paul: Apostle of the Free Spirit.* Carlisle: Paternoster, 1977.

Cann, R. et al., "Mitochondrial DNA and Human Evolution." *Nature.* 325 (1987) 31-36.

Cleere, Henry "Ironmaking." In *Roman Crafts.* edited by Donald Strong and David Brown, 126-41. London: Duckworth, 1976.

Crabbe, Larry. *Understanding People: Deep Longings for Relationship.* Grand Rapids: Zondervan, 1987.

David-Neel, Alexandra. *Magic and Mystery in Tibet.* London: Transworld, 1971.

Dunn, J. D. G. *The Theology of Paul the Apostle.* Edinburgh: T & T Clark, 1998.

Durham, John I. *Word Biblical Commentary, Vol 3, Exodus.* Waco, Texas: Word, 1987.

Eisler, Ivan. "Family Models of Eating Disorders." In *Handbook of Eating Disorders: Theory, Treatment and Research,* edited by George Szmukler et al., 155-76. Chichester: John Wiley & Sons Ltd., 1995.

Evans, Mary. *Prophets of the Lord.* London: Paternoster, 1992.

Farnell, F David. "The Gift of Prophecy in the Old & New Testaments." *Bibliotheca Sacra* 149 (1992) 387-410.

Fee, Gordon D. *God's Empowering Presence.* Peabody, Mass: Hendrickson, 1994

Ferguson, Andrew. *Health: The Strength to be Human.* Leicester: Inter-Varsity, 1993.

Fichter, M. M., and K. M. Pirke. "Starvation Models and Eating Disorders." In *Handbook of Eating Disorders: Theory, Treatment & Research,* edited by George Szmukler et al., 83-107. Chichester: John Wiley & Sons Ltd., 1995.

Fleming, Daniel E. "The Etymological Origins of the Hebrew *nābî*': The One Who Invokes God." *Catholic Biblical Quarterly* 55 (1993) 217-24.

Forster, E. S. *The Works of Aristotle: Problemata. Vol 7*. Oxford: Oxford University Press, 1927.
Frend, W H C. *The Early Church*. London: SCM, 1982.
Gallagher, Bernard J. III. *The Sociology of Mental Illness*. Englewood Cliffs: Prentice-Hall, 1995.
Gaskell, Deborah. "Weighing in on Slimming Drugs." *Chemistry in Britain* 34.8 (1998) 41–45.
Gilbert, Paul. *Counselling for Depression*. London: Sage Publications, 1992.
Goodman, Neil. "The Serotonergic System and Mysticism: Could LSD and the Nondrug-Induced Mystical Experience Share Common Neural Mechanisms?" *Journal of Psychoactive Drugs* 34.3 (2002) 263–72.
Hamilton, Victor P. *The Book of Genesis: Chapters 18–50*. Grand Rapids: Wm. B Eerdmans, 1995.
Harrison, R. K. *Introduction to the Old Testament*. London: Tyndale, 1970.
Hobson, J. Allan. *Dreaming: An Introduction to the Science of Sleep*. New York: Oxford University Press, 2002.
Hui, Archie. "The Spirit of Prophecy and Pauline Pneumatology." *Tyndale Bulletin* 50.1 (1999) 93–115.
James, Barry J. and Samuels, Curtis A. "High Stress Life Events and Spiritual Development." *Journal of Psychology and Theology*. 27.3 (1999) 250–60.
Lacocque, André, and Pierre-Emmanuel Lacocque. *Jonah: A Psycho-Religious Approach to the Prophet*. Columbia: University of South Carolina Press, 1990.
Leonard, Brian E. *Fundamentals of Psychopharmacology*. Chichester: John Wiley & Sons, 1997.
Lewis, Rob and Wynne Evans. *Chemistry*. London: Macmillan, 1997.
Lincoln, Andrew T. *Word Biblical Commentary—Ephesians*. Dallas: Word, 1990.
Lynch, Sean. "Chronic Fatigue Syndrome." *Adv Psychiatr Treat* 1 (1994) 33–40.
Marcus, David. "Nineveh's "Three Days' Walk" (Jonah 3:3): Another Interpretation." In *On the Way to Nineveh: Studies in Honour of George M. Landes*, edited by Stephen L. Cook and S. C. Winter, 42–53. Atlanta: Scholars, 1999.
Markus, A. C. et al., *Psychological Problems in General Practice*. Oxford: Oxford University Press, 1989.
Morris, Leon. *The 1st & 2nd Epistles to the Thessalonians*. Grand Rapids: Eerdmans, 1959.
Murphy, Michael, and Steven Donovan. *The Physical and Psychological Effects of Meditation: A Review of Contemporary Research with a Comprehensive Bibliography*. edited by Eugene Taylor. Sausalito, California: Institute of Noetic Sciences, 1997.
Payne, Leanne. *Restoring the Christian Soul—Through Healing Prayer*. Eastbourne: Kingsway, 1992.
Penney, John. "The Testing of New Testament Prophecy." *Journal of Pentecostal Theology* 10 (1997) 35–84.
Reed-Hill, Robert E and Reza Abbaschian. *Physical Metallurgy Principles*. Boston: PWS, 1994.
Routledge, Robin "'An Evil Spirit from the Lord'—Demonic Influence or Divine Instrument." *Evangelical Quarterly* 70.1 (1998) 3–22.
Russell, Colin A. *Cross-currents—Interactions between Science and Faith*. Leicester: Inter-Varsity, 1985.

Schluederberg, A. et al., "An Examination of the Working Case Definition of Chronic Fatigue Syndrome." *American Journal of Medicine* 100.1 (1996) 56–64.

Thalbourne, Michael A., et al., "Transliminality: Its Nature and Correlates." *Journal of the Society for Psychical Research* 91 (1997) 305–31.

Van't Hof, Sonja. *Anorexia Nervosa: The Historical and Cultural Specificity*. Lisse: Swets & Zeitlinger, 1994.

Vogel, Gerald W., et al., "Improvement of Depression by REM Sleep Deprivation." *Archives of General Psychiatry* 37 (1980) 247–53.

Von Rad, Gerhard. *Genesis: A Commentary*. London: SCM, 1972.

Wanamaker, Charles A. *The Epistles to the Thessalonians*. Grand Rapids: Eerdmans, 1990.

Wax, Murray L. "Interpreting Dreams: Joseph, Freud and the Judaic Tradition," *Journal of Psychology and Judaism*. 22.1 (1998) 21–32.

Wilson, David C. "The Significance of Psychophysiological Factors in Prophecy: A Critical Examination of Altered States of Consciousness and Spiritual Encounter in Selected Passages of the Hebrew Bible." PhD diss., University of Manchester, 2006.

Wimber, John and Springer, Kevin. *Power Healing*. London: Hodder & Stoughton, 1986.

www.ingramcontent.com/pod-product-compliance
Lightning Source LLC
Chambersburg PA
CBHW071434160426
43195CB00013B/1890